THE BATTLE OF PICKETT'S MILL

THE BATTLE OF
PICKETT'S MILL

ALONG THE DEAD-LINE

BRAD BUTKOVICH

Charleston · London

THE
History
PRESS

Published by The History Press
Charleston, SC 29403
www.historypress.net

Cover: The Battle of Pickett's Mill. *Painting by Rick Reeves.*

First published 2013

Manufactured in the United States

ISBN 978.1.62619.042.9

Library of Congress CIP data applied for.

To my wife, Holley, without whom I never would have come this far.

Contents

Contents

Preface

This is an account of the Battle of Pickett's Mill, which was fought during the Atlanta Campaign of 1864 on May 27 along the New Hope Church Line in Paulding County, Georgia. Fought in heavy underbrush and difficult terrain, this engagement was short but fierce and left an indelible impression on many of the participants. The battle temporarily halted the Union's attempt to turn the right flank of the Confederate Army of Tennessee. Afterward, the fighting would concentrate around the town of Dallas for a few days at the western end of the line. Only then would the Union armies again try to move east in force.

However, they did not fight in the ravines and ridges along Pickett's Mill Creek in a vacuum. The day before the battle saw the Union divisions struggle to get into position to attack the end of the Confederate line only to discover that it extended far to the east. These maneuvers strongly influenced the decisions made by those in the high command of the Union army, namely General William T. Sherman. The morning and early afternoon on the day of the battle was filled with sharp skirmishing, mistakes and struggling to march thousands of men through the impossible terrain of rural Georgia while keeping some semblance of order. Previous histories of the battles along the Dallas line have simplified the movements of these two days. I have chosen to chronicle them in depth in order to give a better understanding to why the battle ended up being fought where it was.

Like most Civil War battles, Pickett's Mill generated its share of controversies. First and foremost remains General Oliver O. Howard's decision to send his brigades in to attack one at a time. Why he did so and what other options could he have exercised are examined in detail. I also look into other questions, such as why General Nathaniel C. McLean failed to support the right flank of the attack and why Colonel Benjamin F. Scribner's brigade had such a difficult time defeating the dismounted cavalry to his front.

In the grand scheme of the war, the battle was fairly small. However, the two sides fought in a relatively compact area, and the forces engaged at any one time were only a fraction of those present, particularly for the Union army. What the battle lacked in men it more than made up for in intensity. General William B. Hazen, whose men led the initial attack, called the battle "the most fierce, bloody, and persistent assault by our troops in the Atlanta campaign." Such a small, intense battle deserves a narrative from the ground up. Accounts from the participants themselves, privates to generals, form the heart of the story. I examine the movements of the units involved at all levels, sometimes down to the skirmish lines and individual companies. The small size of the battle allows me to do this without dragging the account down into the minutiae of the fight and losing sight of the "big picture."

In many ways, the units themselves are as much a living, breathing entity as the soldiers. The regiments, brigades and divisions each had a proud history and lineage, many stretching back to the beginning of the war. Casualties, hard marching and expired enlistments forced the consolidations of many of these organizations, and each developed its own sense of pride and *esprit de corps* among its members. Therefore, given the small size of the engagement, I decided to go into a little more detail of the history of the brigades and divisions that fought the battle, as well as their commanders. A detailed history of each regiment is still beyond the scope of this book, but I mention highlights in the text where it enhances the flow of the narrative.

As human beings, our understanding of history occurs on many levels. We process information from the text that we read, as well as visually through pictures. I believe that it is absolutely essential to provide a visual anchor to the narrative through the use of detailed maps and pictures of the battlefield. I have filled the book with maps of the movements of the armies the day before the battle, as well as detailed maps of the fight itself. As yet, no one has published a history of the battle in such detail.

Above all, I want to bring to life the story of the men who fought and died for their beliefs in the hot and humid North Georgia wilderness that afternoon. Battles are not just symbols on a map, and we should not view them as such. Men of flesh and blood, with their own desires, strengths and weaknesses struggled that day to fulfill what they thought was their duty to God, country and their fellow soldiers. The men in the ranks, limited in their understanding of what was happening around them by their sense of sight and sound, soon found themselves called upon to test the limits of their endurance. They relied on their officers to make the right decisions and lead them to victory. Some of these leaders, such as General Patrick R. Cleburne, rose to the occasion. His preparations before the battle and skillful direction during it ensured a Union defeat. Others like General McLean would fail miserably, and he found himself relieved of command several days after the battle.

Acknowledgements

This book is my first effort at writing a Civil War history. As such, I owe thanks to a number of people who have helped me along the way. It has been an incredible journey, and I wouldn't have been able to make it without the generosity and kindness of others.

First I would like to thank Scott Mingus Sr., a friend and Civil War author who specializes in the Gettysburg Campaign and actions around York, Pennsylvania. I contacted Scott asking if he had any advice for a first-time author. Not only did he provide several well-informed suggestions, but he also graciously offered to copyedit my manuscript. In addition, Scott offered to provide any cover or interior text I thought would be useful. He set a model for charity that I hope to emulate should a future author seek my help.

I would not have been able to write about the battle if it had not been for the support and help of James Wooten, the interpretive ranger at Pickett's Mill Historic Site. Over the three years of research and writing it took to complete the manuscript, James provided unlimited access to the park, including many areas not normally open to the public. This access was indispensible in re-creating the road network and terrain of the area as it existed during the battle. In addition, he opened up the library at the visitors' center and allowed me to search through the extensive collection, which is fairly complete considering the small size of the battle. He read over the finished manuscript and provided additional insights that he thought were key components of the campaign. Most importantly, we spent hours in conversation during which he continually challenged me to support my conclusions, which did much to lead to the extensive footnoting at the end of the book.

Finally, I would like to dedicate this book to my wife, Holley, for without her love and continued support, it would not have been possible to finish. For over a decade, she has pushed me to follow my dream to write and publish a book—any book. She has put up with my long absences for hours and even days as I traveled to numerous parks and battlefields searching for sources and studying the events more than a century past. She read the manuscript (even though I know she finds it dry and not particularly interesting) and even helped me edit the text. She offered several suggestions to help me focus the narrative along the way. I can't think of a more dedicated and loyal partner to whom I could dedicate this work.

Introduction

The new or casual reader of Civil War history soon finds himself bombarded with a confusing array of new vocabulary words such as regiment, brigade and corps. They all seem to fit together somehow, but quite often it can take several reads of the material to understand them, and even that's not a certainty! The smallest basic maneuver element in Civil War armies was the company, which at full strength had one hundred men but by 1864 averaged between just twenty and sixty soldiers. Companies were assigned a designation based on the alphabet from A to K, with no J. The letter "J" looked too much like the letter "I" when written. A company was commanded by a captain. One important role of a company was to act on detached service as a skirmish line, which was essentially a thin line of men to protect the regiment from being surprised and to likewise gather what information they could from the enemy. Ten companies comprised a regiment, commanded by a colonel, with a lieutenant colonel and major on his staff. The regiment was the basic tactical unit on the battlefield. States gave them a numerical designation, such as the 15th Ohio or the 10th Texas. Each regiment received one or more flags, or colors, that they carried into battle. These colors served the practical purpose of identifying the center of the regiment and as a rallying point. They were also a sense of unit pride, and as foreign as it may seem to modern sentiments, men were more than willing to die in order to keep them aloft or deny their capture by the enemy.

Several regiments assigned together became a brigade, commanded by a brigadier general. If the general fell ill or was wounded in action and unable to continue in command, the senior regimental colonel in the brigade would take command. The Confederate army was very quick to give stars to colonels leading their brigades or assign brigadier generals from elsewhere—the Union army much less so. Colonels could command brigades in the Union army for a very long time, and Congress was very slow to approve promotions. Two or more brigades formed a division, normally commanded by a major general in both armies. Two or more divisions became a corps. With the exception of Lieutenant General Ulysses S. Grant, major general was the highest grade to which a Union officer could rise. Therefore, two-star generals commanded corps and even armies. This was not the case in the Confederacy, where lieutenant generals led corps and two or more corps formed an army, commanded by a full general.

The Federal government named Union armies after the administrative military department from which they originated. The Army of the Cumberland was administratively based out of the Department of the Cumberland, which normally centered around Nashville and the Cumberland River area. The Confederates named their armies after their area of operation. The Army of Northern Virginia fought most of its battles in and around the northern half of the state, and the Army of Tennessee was organized and fought most of its early battles in that state.

A quick note about unit names and designations: by mid-war, casualties and attrition had whittled down regiments to a mere shadow of their former selves. The Union army favored raising new regiments, which was more often a political decision of the state governors. By 1864, Union army commanders were often stuffing six, seven and even nine smaller regiments together in a single brigade. The Confederacy took the more practical step of consolidating small regiments. This led to designations such as the 17th & 18th Texas (Consolidated). In the narrative, I have dropped the "Consolidated" for easy reading. In the unique cases in which infantry and cavalry regiments found themselves consolidated, I have dropped the "Cavalry" designation also. The order of battle at the end of the book provides the complete and formal designations.

At the brigade level and above, Federal armies assigned numbers to their units, such as the First Brigade or Second Division. In their official reports and post-war writings, the officers and men more often than not wrote out the entire number, such as "First" or "Third," so I use those terms throughout the book. This also applies to Union Corps. I favor the use of the written numerical designation at the corps level and do not use the otherwise popular Roman numerals. It flows better, and if writing the full number of the corps was good enough for the generals themselves, it's good enough for me. Confederate units, on the other hand, took the name of their commanding officer as their official designation. For example, you will see names such as Granbury's Brigade or Polk's Corps. Since the terms "brigade" and "division" are part of the formal name of the unit in those instances, they are capitalized, whereas references to a Union formation by its commander's name are not.

A large number of Kentucky and Tennessee volunteers flocked to the Union cause. Despite its southern ties, many more Kentuckians fought for the Union than the Confederacy. So did a surprising number of East Tennesseans, whose portion of the state remained strongly pro-Union throughout the war. The Washington government organized these volunteers into regiments just like any other state. There were no Confederate Kentucky regiments engaged at Pickett's Mill, so to avoid having to add a clumsy looking Union or Confederate designation, assume that all Kentucky regiments named in the book belonged to the Union army. The same cannot be said of Tennessee, as the state had regiments engaged on both sides. However, the Unionists distinguished themselves from their Confederate counterparts by giving regiments the designation East Tennessee. In this book, Tennessee regiments refer to Confederate units, while East Tennessee regiments refer to Union.

Place names are another tricky hazard for the historian. Landmarks such as roads or creeks often did not have names. The soldiers who wrote their reports, letters and diaries may have heard the name of a landmark from a local, and two different soldiers often referred to the same place by different names! The men often called the battle around the Pickett farm New Hope, confusing it with the battle two days previous. Whenever possible, I have used names of terrain features and roads as they were in 1864.

Time is yet another confusing piece of the Civil War puzzle. Keeping track of time was very subjective during the Civil War. Few soldiers or even officers had watches. Those officers who did have watches were generally higher-level field officers—colonels and generals. The time the watches gave was unreliable, not because of poor construction but because there was no standard time synchronization. An officer might set his watch to a local town clock or another officer, which in turn could be different from an officer in another unit. Add to this the fact that the watch would run down and need rewinding, throwing off an accurate time even more, and the problem modern historians have piecing together chronological events becomes clear. Reconciling the conflicting times provided by different officers can be a challenge. When the timing of an event is in doubt, I made a best estimate based on the reports of multiple participants, with a more lengthy explanation provided in the endnotes.

Chapter 1

The Campaign Begins

By the spring of 1864, the Union army had a strong commander-in-chief in the form of Lieutenant General Ulysses S. Grant, and with him, a unified sense of strategy and purpose. No longer would armies in Virginia, Tennessee, Louisiana and other theaters of the war conduct operations according to their own timelines and schedules. Instead, the combined might of the U.S.'s military would advance against the Confederate armies arrayed against them simultaneously. This coordination would prevent one Confederate army from reinforcing the other, as had happened at such places as Bull Run at the beginning of the war, outside of Richmond during the Seven Days' Battles and most notably at Chickamauga in September 1863. At the same time, it would stretch Confederate logistics and resources to their limit as the fledgling nation struggled to confront an array of invaders across its boundaries.

In early May, two great armies were poised to strike the main blows against the Confederacy. One, the Army of the Potomac commanded by Major General George G. Meade, would advance across Virginia and bring his counterpart, General Robert E. Lee and his Army of Northern Virginia, to battle. Grant would travel with the Army of the Potomac and keep it on a tight leash.

The other army, centered in Chattanooga, Tennessee, and the surrounding area, would march through North Georgia. Its objective was to destroy the Confederate defenders confronting it and capture the city of Atlanta along the way. In fact, this Union force was comprised of three armies. Major General George H. Thomas commanded the Army of the Cumberland, the largest of the three. The next largest was the Army of the Tennessee under Major

General James B. McPherson, with barely a third the number of men as the larger army. The smallest army was the Army of the Ohio commanded by Major General John M. Schofield. It was barely an army at all, consisting of only one small infantry corps and one cavalry division. The overall commander of these three armies, collectively known as the Military Division of the Mississippi, was Major General William T. Sherman. All together, the three armies had 110,123 men between them.[1] Confederate General Joseph E. Johnston and the 54,500 men of his Army of Tennessee[2] (not to be confused with McPherson's similarly named Army of *the* Tennessee) were just as equally determined to stop them from marching any farther into the Confederacy.

The campaign for Georgia began in earnest on May 7 when the three Union armies approached the Confederate army stationed along Rocky Face Ridge outside of Dalton. There, the Army of the Cumberland and the Army of the Ohio faced off against the Army of Tennessee. Unknown to Johnston, however, Sherman had no intention of sending his men up the steep slopes of the ridge into the sights of the entrenched Confederates. He sent McPherson and his Army of the Tennessee south through the valley of Snake Creek and Snake Creek Gap to capture the town of Resaca on the Western & Atlantic Railroad. This railroad, running from Atlanta to Chattanooga, was the supply lifeline of both armies. On May 9, McPherson's army emerged from Snake Creek Gap and threatened Resaca but retreated to the gap without capturing it. Realizing the danger, Johnston abandoned Rocky Face Ridge and concentrated his army, as well as reinforcements on their way from Mississippi, at the town. Sherman followed, and the two opponents fought a two-day battle around the town on May 15 and 16. Both sides made heavy use of earthworks and entrenchments for protection. Johnston withdrew only when Sherman threatened the railroad by crossing the Oostanaula River south of town.

After marching south, Johnston next drew his army into position outside of the small town of Cassville. There, on May 19, the two sides once again confronted each other, but the Confederates withdrew during the night because Johnston feared his entrenchments were poorly built and subject to crossfire from enemy artillery. He continued retreating south of the next geographical obstacle, the Etowah River, and took up a formidable defensive position around Allatoona Pass, a deep gorge cut through a hill in the Allatoona Mountains for the passage of the Western & Atlantic. After approaching and securing passages over the Etowah, Sherman spent the next two days resting his armies, building up supplies and getting his men into position for the next phase of the campaign.

Chapter 2

A Few Days' Rest

I t was a warm day in May, and Andrew Gleason was singing under the shade of live oak trees. Three years of civil war had brought the Union army into Georgia and the heartland of the Confederate States of America.[3] Sergeant Major Gleason was a member of the 15th Ohio Infantry Regiment, and he and his comrades spent the three days along the Etowah resting, preparing twenty days worth of three-fifths rations and holding religious services on Sunday. The services featured a cadre of singers that Gleason, who had studied music in Chicago before the war, had originally organized in September 1861. They had been entertaining the regiment ever since. Originally a private in Company H, he had risen in the ranks as the war dragged on.

The 15th Ohio, led by Colonel William Wallace, shared membership in its brigade with five other regiments. These were the 35th and 89th Illinois, the 32nd Indiana, the 49th Ohio and the 15th Wisconsin. Colonel William H. Gibson commanded the brigade. Gibson was born in Cross Creek Township, Ohio, in 1822, but his family moved to Seneca County when young William was four months old. As he grew up, he studied debate, carpentry and law, eventually beginning his own practice in Tiffin in 1843. A staunch Whig, he campaigned for Zachary Taylor in 1848 and was a delegate for Winfield Scott at the Whig National Convention in 1852. When the Whig party disintegrated, he became a Republican and won the election for Ohio State Treasurer in 1856. Unfortunately, a scandal involving a shortfall of funds caused by his predecessor marred his tenure as treasurer. Though cleared of any financial wrongdoing, an investigating commission found Gibson guilty of trying to cover up the extent of the damage. He resigned under a cloud of suspicion in 1857.[4] Determined to prove himself when war came in 1861, he spent the first months recruiting men for Lincoln's first call for troops. However, when these inexperienced soldiers proved unable to suppress the Rebellion, Gibson resolved to take a more active role. On July 25, he had a large recruiting poster printed and published, calling on the men of northern Ohio to join him in the cause.[5] By mid-August, he had a regiment assembled, the 49th Ohio Infantry, and a colonel's commission. He led the 49th at Shiloh (where he was wounded), Stone's River, Chickamauga, up Missionary Ridge and into the heart of Georgia. He had often led his brigade when the commanding officer was absent and proved to be a well-liked leader. He knew how to give a few inspirational words before leading men into battle but could also relate to the men on a more personal level, even participating in practical jokes. Such familiarity didn't seem to harm his reputation or ability to command.[6] When the popular brigade commander Brigadier General August Willich was wounded at Resaca, Gibson took command of the First Brigade, Third Division of the Fourth Army Corps. The corps was in camp outside of Cassville.

Captain George W. Lewis of Company B, 124th Ohio, spent the time resting his men and admiring the fertile and productive valley of the Etowah.[7] Elected to lead the company at its inception in the summer of 1862, Lewis had seen it through its training and true baptism of fire at Chickamauga. Now, after two weeks of marching and fighting, all eyes were on the next phase of the campaign. The 124th Ohio, brigaded with seven other regiments, comprised the Second Brigade, Third Division. They were the 1st, 41st and 93rd Ohio, the 5th, 6th and 23rd Kentucky and the 6th Indiana. Their brigade commander was the tough, no-nonsense Brigadier General William B. Hazen. Hazen was born in Vermont in 1830 but grew up in Hiram, Ohio. A West Point graduate in the class of 1855, he served as a second lieutenant in the 4th U.S. Infantry in the Pacific Northwest and then later with the 8th U.S. Infantry in Texas. In October 1859, he and a mixed party of soldiers and civilians pursued a group of Indians accused of killing two civilians near Sabinal. They caught up to them on November 3. In the ensuing firefight, they killed the Indians, but Hazen was shot. The ball passed through his hand, fractured the metacarpal bone of the ring finger and lodged in his side. Returning east, the war began in 1861 while he was recovering from his wound. He arrived at Bull Run in July, too late to participate in the battle, but he did get caught in the mass of routed troops fleeing back to Washington, D.C.[8] Afterward, he received his commission as colonel of the 41st Ohio Infantry but began commanding a new brigade in January 1862. He led his brigade at Shiloh, Perryville, and stopped the momentum of the Confederate attack at Stone's River at the Round Forest. The fighting at the Round Forest earned him his brigadier's star. With the Confederates pouring through a breach in the center of the Union lines on the first day of Chickamauga, he sacrificed the men of his brigade in order to buy the time necessary to organize reinforcements into a line that could close the gap. It worked. On the second day of the battle, he coolly led his men in the defense of their positions at multiple points on the battlefield. At Chattanooga, he led his newly merged brigade on a daring surprise attack down the Tennessee River that was instrumental in opening the supply lines into the city. Following his men up the slopes of Missionary Ridge in their spontaneous charge, he laid claim to being the first unit to reach the top. It was a claim, of course, that the egos of future postwar veterans would not allow to stand uncontested. The brigade began the current campaign with 2,443 men but so far had seen relatively little combat.[9] Sporting a handlebar mustache and a soul patch extending below his chin, the man seen as "aggressive, arrogant, tyrannical, honorable, truthful, courageous—a skillful soldier, a faithful friend, and one of the most exasperating of men"[10] would face one of his greatest challenges among the ravines and ridges of North Georgia.

Over in the Third Brigade's bivouac, First Lieutenant Marcus Woodcock of Company B, 9th Kentucky, took an opportunity on May 22 to write a letter back home. "I would either go to Atlanta or get a whipping ere I wrote another," he wrote, and as he admitted after the war, it came closer to coming true than he anticipated. That Sunday, officers ordered the regiment to pack up all unnecessary baggage and send it back to Chattanooga by rail. Also, twenty days worth of rations were cooked and loaded into the wagons. Something definitely "was up."[11] Similar preparations were underway in the other regiments of the brigade. In addition to the 9th, the 17th Kentucky represented Union hearts in Bluegrass country. Nearby were the 13th, 19th and 59th Ohio and the 79th and 86th Indiana. The brigade was commanded by Brigadier General Samuel Beatty, but Beatty was currently sick and handed command of the unit over to Colonel Frederick Knefler of the 79th Indiana the next morning. Unlike the division's other two brigade commanders, Knefler was a first-generation Jewish-Hungarian immigrant, and he had quite an adventurous life before the war. Born in Arad, Hungary, in 1833 to a prominent physician, Knefler joined the revolutionary army during Hungary's 1848–49 War of Liberation against the Hapsburg Empire. Following the revolutionary's defeat, the family fled the country and immigrated to America in 1850. Settling in Indianapolis,

Brigadier General William B. Hazen. *Courtesy of National Archives.*

his father helped found the Indianapolis Hebrew Congregation, the city's first synagogue, in 1856. Knefler worked as a carpenter and studied law, along the way making a lifelong friend in Lew Wallace, future author of *Ben-Hur*. When the war began, he joined Wallace's 11th Indiana, rising to the rank of captain and seeing action at Fort Donelson and Shiloh. Appointed colonel of the new 79th Indiana in August 1862, his men saw him as a strict disciplinarian but came to respect him after their baptism of fire. He led the regiment through Stone's River, Chickamauga and Chattanooga. On the first day of Chickamauga, he led the regiment in the capture of an artillery battery. On the second, he was swept from the field when half the regiment routed in the Confederate assault and the other half rallied and stood fast on Horseshoe Ridge. General Beatty praised his bravery at Missionary Ridge, and a fellow colonel even recommended him for a brigadier's commission. Now six months later, he found himself leading the brigade. Lieutenant Colonel Samuel P. Oyler would take the reins of the 79th.[12]

Like many of the units in the Army of the Cumberland, the division was an amalgamation of units worn from combat and hard service—in this case, three different previous divisions. Merged after Chickamauga, Gibson's and Hazen's brigades comprised the remnants of two divisions. One division had been overrun at Stone's River and roughly handled at Chickamauga, while the other had fought to distinction at Round Forest at the former and stood fast at the latter. After their merger, they bonded into a cohesive force, sharing in the suffering during the siege of Chattanooga and exhilarating in the victorious charge up the slopes of Missionary Ridge. Gibson's brigade was unique in another aspect: orders given by bugle were sounded by German bugle calls that General Willich had used in Germany during the 1848 revolution. Hence, the Rebels couldn't recognize the otherwise familiar bugle notes. Knefler's seven regiments had served in the same division together for most of the war, though in two separate brigades until after Chickamauga. Unfortunately, their record was spotty at best. While they were victorious on the second day of Shiloh, they were overwhelmed and forced to retreat from their positions on both days of Stone's River. Likewise at Chickamauga, the Confederates routed the two brigades of the division from the field on both days of the battle. After their merger, led by General Beatty, they scaled Missionary Ridge and helped break the siege of Chattanooga.

The guiding hand of the Third Division, Fourth Army Corps, to which the three brigades belonged, was Brigadier General Thomas J. Wood. There was hardly a division commander in the army with more to prove. Short and slim with a dark complexion and black whiskers, he had a talent for profanity and the ability to "blow his own horn."[13] Born in Munfordville, Kentucky, in 1823, he graduated from West Point in 1845. He won a brevet promotion (a temporary increase in grade, responsibility and stature without an increase in pay) at Buena Vista during the Mexican War and afterward saw service with the cavalry on the frontier. At the beginning of the war, Wood helped organize and train several Indiana regiments, which earned him a brigadier general's star in October 1861. He commanded a division at Shiloh and was instrumental in shoring up the torn Federal line at Stone's River.[14] His division fought hard on the first day of Chickamauga, but on the second day, he led his division away from its place in the line under a direct order from army headquarters—this despite the fact that his skirmishers were actively engaged with the enemy to his front. Many thought he had been publicly berated by the commander of the army for failure to follow orders promptly twice before and that he was determined to avoid a third time. Wood publicly denied that at least one of those instances had actually occurred. In addition, a corps commander was present when Wood received the order to move, and he gave permission to carry out the order. Unfortunately, the Confederates attacked the gap before new arrivals could close it and routed the center and right of the Union army from the field.[15] Wood's division, however, remained, aiding in the famous defense of Snodgrass Hill. Escaping permanent censure because the order to move was in writing, Wood kept his command and redeemed himself by following the men of his division up Missionary Ridge two months later, although he was initially more concerned with how it would damage his career if the unauthorized assault failed. Sometimes though, success has its own rewards, whether intentional or not, and Wood's career as a division commander continued. So far, the campaign had not seriously tested Wood and the 8,180 men he left Chattanooga with.

Camped nearby were the other two divisions of the Fourth Corps. Major General David S. Stanley commanded the First Division and Brigadier General John Newton the Third. The Fourth Corps was created in October 1863 by merging together the Twentieth and Twenty-First Corps. After Chickamauga, the regiments in the Army of the Cumberland were skeletons of their former selves, and so by extension, were their brigades. The mergers were necessary in order to bring brigade strengths back up and make them into viable maneuver elements. The Fourteenth Corps of the Army was large enough that it could consolidate its own divisions and still retain its corps designation, although it did absorb brigades from the Reserve Corps. The Twentieth and Twenty-First Corps were not so fortunate. Each was smaller than the Fourteenth to begin with, and it was obvious that the only way to achieve a comparable strength with the Fourteenth would be to merge them. The new corps was designated the Fourth Army Corps, recycling a number from a corps deactivated that August.[16] The troops fought under their new organization as they lifted the siege of Chattanooga and pushed the Confederates off Missionary Ridge. In April 1864, Major General Oliver O. Howard took command of the corps.[17]

Howard was in a distinctive minority among those serving in the forces assembled in North Georgia. He was an "easterner," having transferred from the Army of the Potomac in Virginia to help shore up the Army of the

Cumberland after the debacle of Chickamauga. Born in Leeds, Maine, in 1830, he graduated from Bowdoin College at the age of nineteen and entered West Point. He graduated fourth in his class in 1854. After a few pedestrian assignments, he transferred to Florida in January 1857 and participated in the Third Seminole War. He saw no combat but while stationed in Tampa converted to Methodism. He would remain an ardent Christian for the remainder of his life. While his contemporaries in the Civil War often mentioned his strong faith, Howard's description in his autobiography is very matter-of-fact on the subject.[18] He was also a devoted teetotaler who never drank alcohol. In September 1857, the army recalled him to West Point to become an instructor, promoting him to first lieutenant. After war broke out, the men of the newly formed 3rd Maine Infantry elected him colonel. At the First Battle of Bull Run, he exercised temporary command of his brigade, and in September 1861, he became a brigadier general and took permanent command of the brigade. Wounded twice at the Battle of Fair Oaks in June 1862, doctors were forced to amputate his left arm. Recovering quickly, he led a brigade at Antietam and a division at Fredericksburg.

In April 1863, Howard took command of the Eleventh Corps. At Chancellorsville that May, his corps held the extreme right of the Union line. Howard deployed the corps with its flank "up in the air"—not anchored or protected by any natural terrain feature nor bent back or refused to protect it from a flank attack. Howard refused to change the disposition of his men despite repeated reports from skirmishers and pickets that a force of Confederates was moving past the end of the line, claiming that his corps "was by positive orders riveted to that position" by the army commander.[19] In the late afternoon, a Confederate corps led by Thomas "Stonewall" Jackson burst out of the wood line at the end of the Union line, crushing the Eleventh Corps and changing the course of the battle. At Gettysburg, Howard took command of the field on the first day of battle and oversaw the defenses of Cemetery Hill, leaving command of the Eleventh to the senior division commander. Unfortunately, the Confederates drove the Eleventh from the fields north of town. Unfairly or not, soldiers and commanders throughout the rest of the Army of the Potomac blamed Howard.

The Lincoln administration responded to the Union defeat at Chickamauga that September with alacrity. While Grant's Army of the Tennessee at Vicksburg hurried reinforcements toward Chattanooga, the Eleventh and Twelfth Corps headed west from Virginia. In a remarkable feat of logistics, the two corps loaded onto trains, travelled 1,200 miles and arrived on the banks of the Tennessee River in a week.[20] The easterners

Major General Oliver O. Howard. *Courtesy of National Archives.*

helped to open the overland route to the beleaguered city, capture Lookout Mountain in late November and drive the Confederates from Missionary Ridge. In April 1864, while organizing his armies for the upcoming campaign, Sherman merged the Eleventh and Twelfth Corps to form a new Twentieth Corps for much the same reasons as the creation of the Fourth. Command of the Twentieth went to Major General Joseph Hooker, as Sherman offered Howard command of the Fourth. Sherman thought well of Howard, writing, "He is very honest, sincere and moral even to piety, but brave, having lost an arm already."[21] So far in the campaign, the Fourth Corps had delivered a mediocre performance. An attack by Newton's Second Division along Rocky Face Ridge at the beginning of the campaign had stalled, mostly due to the difficult terrain. At Resaca, the Confederates drove Stanley's First Division from its position, but a counterattack from the Twentieth Corps stabilized the lines.[22] However, it should be noted that no other Federal units had thus far achieved a decisive breakthrough during the campaign, and the Confederates had thrice retreated from entrenched positions. For the first time in two weeks, the Federals north of the Etowah River didn't have to worry about dodging artillery shells or fear the dull thud of a sharpshooter's bullet striking flesh. Most of the time, they were able to relax in camp, write letters home and, in many cases, bathe off two weeks of sweat, grime and dust.

General Wood even found time to have a little fun at Howard's expense. While in camp, a group of officers invited Howard into a tent for a drink. He politely refused. "What's the use Howard, of your being so singular," chided Wood. "Come along and have a good time with the rest of us. Why not?" Sherman, who was present, quickly came to Howard's defense. "Wood, let Howard alone!" he said. "I want one officer who don't drink!"[23] Amusing as these moments of levity were, there was still work to do, and nobody was busier then Sherman. Headquartered in a small cottage in Kingston, a few miles west of Cassville, the consummate workaholic had to appraise Washington and Grant of his progress, plan his next move and manage the resupply of his army. He was so busy that he literally lost track of the days. That Sunday morning, while pouring over paperwork, he heard a church bell ringing. Thinking some mischievous soldier was goofing off, he sent a guard to bring in those responsible. A guard brought a disheveled civilian before him. When informed that the man, who turned out to be the Reverend E.P. Smith of the Christian Commission, had rung the bell for Sunday service, he exclaimed, "Sunday, Sunday! Didn't know it was Sunday—let him go."[24]

Sherman kept the War Department in Washington up to date on his progress every evening via telegraph. He knew of Grant's progress in Virginia, including the bloody battles fought in the Wilderness and Spotsylvania. So far, Sherman had avoided the bloody frontal assaults his counterparts in Virginia had been making for weeks. Instead, he had used smaller local attacks and marches around the flanks of his opponent to force them to retreat. Now, the Confederates under Johnston held their strongest position yet. South of the Etowah, the Western & Atlantic Railroad ran through the grandiosely named Allatoona Mountains, though in truth they were little more than a series of steep, rugged hills. Still, they were a formidable obstacle. Four miles below the river, the railroad traversed the hills at Allatoona Pass. The pass was a man-made cut through a hill 175 feet deep and 360 feet long. The Army of Tennessee was camped at the cut and along the hills bordering it, creating a formidable barrier to Sherman's advance south.

Fortunately, Sherman was familiar with the area. As a lieutenant in 1844, he had ridden through the area en route from Marietta, Georgia, to Bellefonte, Alabama. A direct assault would be difficult and likely result in heavy casualties, so he would have to come up with an alternate course of action. He could move to the east, cross the Etowah upstream of the railroad bridge and flank the Confederates out of Allatoona from that direction. Unfortunately, the nature of the Western & Atlantic Railroad made this impractical. West of the railroad bridge, both the river and the railroad angled northwest. If Sherman were to move east, Johnston could swing west, recross the river and cut him off from the railroad and his supply line. Additionally, the farther east and southeast he went, the longer his wagon supply train would be, increasing its vulnerability. That left only a crossing downstream, or to the west of the railroad bridge. Leaving the safety of the tracks, he would march his armies across the river south of Cassville and Kingston and head toward Dallas, fifteen miles to the south. Having outflanked Johnston to the west and avoided the rough terrain around Allatoona, he would then turn east toward Marietta and the railroad.[25] This would force Johnston to retreat and perhaps even trap him by putting the Federals between the Confederate army and Atlanta. There were difficulties to overcome, to be sure. The countryside between the Etowah and Dallas was wilderness in many places, and maps of the area were poor. Supplies would have to be brought to the army by wagon from north of the river until contact was again established with the railroad at Marietta and the tracks cleared of Confederates in between. The key to a successful operation would be careful planning.

First, Sherman made sure that the railroad was repaired and functioning from Chattanooga to Cassville. Second, he lightened his army. They would have to march quickly from the river to Dallas and from there to Marietta in order to catch the Confederates off guard. To accomplish that, he ordered all wounded, sick and worthless idlers sent north to Chattanooga. Next, he further lightened the load of his army by ordering unnecessary baggage and wagons north as well. Cooks were to prepare rations for twenty days and load them into wagons. Each soldier would be issued one pound of bread, flour, or meal; beef on the hoof; sugar; coffee; salt; and two days worth of bacon per week. The horses and mules of the army received four pounds of grain every day. In addition, organized foraging parties sent into the countryside would supplement the rations for both humans and animals. Indiscriminate plunder was prohibited.[26] Finally, Sherman prepared the orders, spelling out to his subordinates exactly what he expected of them. The Army of the Tennessee would leave Kingston and march to Van Wert, west of Dallas, and approach that town from the west. The Army of the Cumberland would leave Cassville and march south along roads west of the village of Burnt Hickory (also known as Huntsville) and enter Dallas from the north. Sherman ordered the Army of the Ohio to move through Burnt Hickory itself and protect the left flank of the army, closest to the Confederates. From there, the combined armies would advance toward Marietta.[27]

The soldiers did their part getting ready. Cooks prepared their rations and loaded them onto wagons. Soldiers packed up unwanted belongings and sent them north. However, not everything went smoothly, and not everybody appreciated the orders to travel light. Brigadier General Richard W. Johnson, commanding the First Division of the Fourteenth Corps, ordered regiments and brigades to turn in their remaining wagons. Armies run on red tape, and this caused delays, forcing regimental officers to carry their essential paperwork in their hats and pockets. Artillerymen griped about orders to reduce even further the baggage carried on their limbers.[28] Despite the gripes, soldiers still found time for amusement. Upon investigating a sting on his leg, a soldier from Indiana discovered a scorpion, which were uncommon up north. The man feared the venom would prove poisonous, but of course it was no more harmful than the sting of a wasp. However, the novelty of the creature and the anecdote proved memorable enough to be included in the regimental history decades later. Some were a bit more contemplative of their surroundings. Private William N. Price of the 6th Tennessee (Union) wrote in his diary, "As my eye wandered over the mighty multitude of men in this pleasant valley, the question arose in my mind how many of this vast assemblage would be so happy as to gain an admittance into that land of rest where war, sin and sorrow never enter and parting from friends is known no more and where Sabbath's never end."[29]

The march south was about to resume.

Chapter 3

To Hurl a Host Back

S outh of the Etowah, the Confederates were also taking advantage of the break. Many, like Thomas J. Stokes of the 10th Texas, took the time to write letters home. Though serving in a Texas regiment, he was actually from Decatur, Georgia, and had moved out west before the war. Five days earlier, his regiment had formed for battle near Rome Crossroads outside of Calhoun on land his family had lived on. "In the valley of my boyhood, I felt as if I could hurl a host back," he wrote. While some may have despaired after retreating several times, Stokes's opinion probably still prevailed. Another soldier wrote, "The Army of Tennessee has been forced to fall back because of Sherman's superiority in numbers. It may turn out for the best—let us trust so in all events. The troops are in fine spirits and eager for a decisive fight."[30]

Joe Johnston was also ready and eager for the decisive fight of the campaign. Unfortunately, he had not been able to bring it about so far. Much of that blame fell to his subordinates, who until now had given him conflicting or false information at critical moments. For example, division commander Major General William H.T. Walker's contradictory account of the Federal's beachhead on the Oostanaula River south of Resaca led to a series of halting counterattacks to the north. Other times, they had simply failed to carry out his orders despite adversity, as was the case of an aborted ambush entrusted to corps commander Lieutenant General John Bell Hood at Cassville. Still, Johnston is not blameless, and he certainly committed his fair share of mistakes. He had failed to ensure that his cavalry commander had adequately posted his forces to prevent the surprise movement of McPherson through Snake Creek Gap. At the beginning of the campaign, he had also failed to destroy a railroad tunnel that would have significantly hindered Sherman's ability to supply the Federal forces south of Chattanooga. While he had destroyed the railroad bridge over the Etowah after retreating south of it, he had failed to burn several bridges to the west. The disposition of his forces south of the Etowah also lacked imagination. Most of his cavalry, commanded by Major General Joseph Wheeler, guarded the fords and crossings upriver to the east, leaving only one division of cavalry keeping an eye on the crossings to the west. His infantry was concentrated in and around Allatoona Pass itself and the immediate area.[31] With the exception of the south side of the river across from the burned railroad bridge itself, he had no plans to strongly oppose any of the crossings with entrenched infantry. Instead, he seemed content to let Sherman's armies cross unopposed and to let his cavalry keep him appraised of the Federal movement, responding accordingly.

Among those waiting to respond were Major General Patrick Ronayne Cleburne and the men of his division. Revered by the troops under his command and highly respected by most of his fellow officers, Cleburne had earned a reputation as a fierce fighter against long odds. The thirty-six-year-old was born in Ireland to a middle-class doctor. After his father's untimely death, he became a physician's apprentice himself at the age of fifteen to help relieve the family's financial troubles. However, he was continually rejected by higher institutions that could further his studies. Faced with no income and the devastating potato blight of 1845–46, he joined the British Army, where he remained for three years. His family, however, could not escape the economic hardship of the famine, and he purchased his release in 1849 so that he could move them to America. Once there, family members went their separate ways and Cleburne settled in the frontier town of Helena, Arkansas. There, he rose rapidly in the community, alternately owning a drugstore and newspaper before finally establishing himself as a successful lawyer. When war broke out, he took the militia company he had helped train in Helena, the Yell Rifles, to the capital of Little Rock, and the men soon elected him colonel of a new regiment. Elevated to brigade command and promoted to brigadier general shortly before the battle of Shiloh in April 1862, he led his men into combat for the first time. By the fall, he had risen to command of a division. On New Year's Eve, his division helped spearhead the opening assault on the Union lines at Stone's River, smashing through position after position until his exhausted men reached the limit of their endurance and could no longer advance after seven hours of continuous combat. On the first day at Chickamauga in September 1863, his men launched a successful night attack, but entrenched Federals stopped them in their tracks the next day. At Missionary Ridge and Ringgold Gap in November, he showed his prowess by leading the men of his division to glory and the accolades of the Confederate government by defending his position against Union troops three times stronger than his. As a gesture of thanks, when Johnston reorganized the army outside Dalton, Georgia, that winter and standardized the look of the regimental battle flags throughout his command, he allowed Cleburne's regiments to keep their distinctive flags. When Union troops saw that their opponents carried blue flags with white borders and white circles in the center, they knew they were up against the best of the best.

Not everybody was happy with Cleburne that winter. Seeing the progress of the war as a simple numbers game that the Confederacy could not win, Cleburne submitted a proposal to the highest ranking officers of the army outlining the arming of the country's slaves and inducting them into the armed forces of the Confederacy in return for their freedom. Despite his best intentions, the proposal was met with skepticism by most and outright hostility by a few. When a copy of the proposal made its way to Confederate president Jefferson Davis, he ordered it suppressed and had everyone who knew about it sworn to secrecy. Despite Cleburne's outstanding combat record, his prospects for promotion seemed slim. But the winter was not entirely grim. In January, he accompanied his corps commander, Lieutenant General William J. Hardee, south to Mobile, Alabama. Hardee had been Cleburne's commanding officer for much of the war, and the two had become very close friends. In Mobile, Cleburne stood up for Hardee as his best man as the latter was married. The mood was catching. Normally awkward and shy among women, Cleburne fell in love at first sight with the maid of honor, twenty-four-year-old Susan Tarleton. They remained constant companions during the trip, and before returning north, he asked her to marry him. She did not answer immediately but gave Cleburne permission to write her. A flurry of letters followed, and during a second trip in March, she relented and happily agreed to the engagement. The spirits of both the division and its commander were understandably high as winter turned to spring and the upcoming campaign season.

Cleburne and his men saw some minor combat at Dug Gap, Resaca, and Rome Crossroads during the opening moves of the new campaign in Georgia but no major assaults or battles. Now his men rested near Willford Mill along Pumpkinvine Creek just west of Allatoona Pass.[32] Taking advantage of the respite, Cleburne took time off to write Susan. His aide, Learned Magnum, a friend and former law partner from Helena, listened as Cleburne would read aloud passages of his letters to her. Magnum noted that the letters were surprisingly "full of a most sweet and tender passion" for a man who had always been ill at ease around women. Unfortunately, while at Allatoona he also received word that his half-brother, Christopher "Kit" Cleburne, was killed on May 10 while raiding through Kentucky with Confederate cavalryman John Hunt Morgan.

Not everyone had time for letters. Private William Austin Smith, a teamster, spent the time caring for his mules and recording in his diary.[33] His regiment, the 48th Tennessee, was part of Polk's Brigade in Cleburne's Division (the Confederates named their brigades, divisions and often corps after their commanders, unlike the numerical designations in the Federal armies). The 35th Tennessee, 5th Confederate and the 1st & 15th Arkansas rounded out the brigade. The dual designation of the Arkansas regiment came about because the two individual regiments had suffered so many casualties that they could no longer function effectively as individual units. Though consolidated into one unit, they retained their individual regimental numbers for morale. This was a common occurrence in the Confederate army. All were tough veterans who had seen combat since Fort Donelson and Shiloh and had taken part in all of the battles of Cleburne's Division. Commanding the brigade was Brigadier General Lucius E. Polk.

Polk was born in Salisbury, North Carolina, but his family moved to Columbia, Tennessee, when he was two. As an adult, Polk attended the University of Virginia for a year before moving to Helena, Arkansas, where he took up farming. In 1861, he marched off to war with the Yell Rifles. The colonel of the company's parent regiment was killed at Shiloh, where Polk was also wounded, and he was elected colonel. When Cleburne advanced from command of the brigade to command of the division, he successfully championed Polk for command of the brigade and a brigadier general's commission. He commanded his brigade through all the subsequent battles of the division, leading his men with skill and courage while gaining a few more wounds to show for it. Polk was very much a protégé of Cleburne's. Private Sam Watkins of Cheatham's Division wrote, "Polk was to Cleburne what Murat or the old guard was to Napoleon."[34] Polk's uncle was Lieutenant General Leonidas Polk, commander of the Army of Mississippi, more commonly referred to as Polk's Corps in its service in Georgia under Joseph Johnston. Regular maintenance and rest were the order of the day in the other brigades of the division. Jeff Fowler of the 3rd Confederate regiment

Major General Patrick Ronayne Cleburne. *Courtesy of Library of Congress.*

noted how clear and warm the days along Pumpkinvine Creek were and how each night he got a good night's sleep.[35] Still, arms and equipment needed to be taken care of. For example, General Hardee ordered that everyone in his corps discharge their weapons at 6:00 a.m. on the 22nd, presumably to ensure that all were in working order and that nobody left wet powder in them (which would render them useless later during battle). There was a constant roar of musketry for about an hour from the other regiments in the brigade, and the rest of the corps as well.[36] The other regiments in the brigade were all from Arkansas: the 2nd & 24th, 5th & 13th, 6th &

37

7th and the 8th & 19th. In truth, the 3rd Confederate began with eight companies from Arkansas and two from Mississippi, but it entered directly into Confederate service and had never been a state regiment. A tough unit from west of the Mississippi River, the brigade had followed Cleburne in most of his battles.

Leading these rough and tumble westerners was a man just as tough, Brigadier General Daniel C. Govan. Like Polk, he was also born in North Carolina, but his family moved to Mississippi when he was three. He graduated from South Carolina College (today's University of South Carolina) in 1848 and the next year was in California looking for his fortune during the Gold Rush. Elected deputy sheriff of Sacramento in 1850, he returned to Mississippi two years later to take up farming. In 1860, he moved to Helena, Arkansas. In 1861, he raised a company of soldiers, was elected lieutenant colonel of the 2nd Arkansas and became its colonel in January 1862. He led his regiment at Shiloh, Perryville, and Stone's River and commanded the brigade at Chickamauga and the battles around Chattanooga when its brigadier was absent. In December 1863, Richmond appointed him a brigadier general and gave him permanent command of the brigade.

Weapons and mules weren't the only things needing upkeep. Captain Samuel T. Foster watched the men of his Company H bathe in Pumpkinvine Creek, while others washed their clothes and built fires. The men then held their clothes over the fires to kill any lice, the bane of any nineteenth-century soldier, as lice tended not to discriminate between enlisted men and officers. Foster also watched his colonel, Franklin C. Wilkes, take off his shirt, turn it inside out and inspect it thoroughly.[37] The rest of the men in the regiment, the 24th & 25th Texas Cavalry (dismounted), likewise performed similar rituals. Presumably, the other regiments of the brigade—the 6th Texas Infantry & 15th Texas Cavalry (dismounted) consolidated regiment, the 7th Texas, the 10th Texas, the 17th & 18th Texas Cavalry (dismounted) and the 24th & 25th Texas Cavalry (dismounted)—did as well. Their mounts had been taken from them earlier in the war for logistical reasons, but the government allowed them to keep their cavalry designation followed by "(dismounted)" to keep up their morale. The brigade had a unique history. Stationed in Arkansas at the beginning of the war, they were captured at Arkansas Post in January 1863 and exchanged months later. No other command wanted former prisoners of war who apparently didn't put up a fight in their ranks—none except Patrick Cleburne, who took the men and formed a new brigade for his division. They didn't make much headway against the Union lines at Chickamauga, who cut their brigadier in half with a cannon shell.

However, they distinguished themselves at Tunnel Hill on Missionary Ridge, where their new brigadier was wounded, and again days later at Ringgold Gap. Led by yet another new brigadier general, Hiram B. Granbury, and reinforced by the transfer into the brigade of other Texas regiments from other commands, the brigade helped stop a Union division from breaking through at Dug Gap in the first days of the Atlanta campaign.

Hiram Granbury was born in Copiah County, Mississippi, in 1831, the son of a Baptist minister. In 1850, he moved to Waco, Texas, where he studied law, was admitted to the bar and served as chief justice of McLennan County, Texas, from 1856 to 1858. When the war began, he raised an infantry company and was elected major of the 7th Texas Infantry in October 1861. He surrendered with the garrison at Fort Donelson in February 1862 but was exchanged in August and promoted to colonel of the regiment the same month. He fought with the regiment in Mississippi during the Vicksburg Campaign before his brigade was transferred east to fight at Chickamauga. In November, the parent brigade of the 7th Texas was broken up, and the regiment transferred to Smith's Brigade. Granbury took command of the brigade after Smith's wounding at Missionary Ridge. In February 1864, Granbury received his brigadier general's commission and permanent command of the brigade.

The fourth and final brigade in Cleburne's Division was a mix of Alabama and Mississippi regiments commanded by Brigadier General Mark P. Lowrey. It was composed of the 16th, 33rd and 45th Alabama and the 32nd and 45th Mississippi regiments. Two of the regiments fought at Shiloh, and the rest fought from Perryville onward. They crushed the Union flank at Stone's River, but poor brigade leadership hampered the command at Chickamauga. Mark Lowrey rose to command the brigade shortly thereafter, and the regiments fought gallantly to hold off the Federals at Tunnel Hill and Ringgold Gap.

Mark P. Lowrey was born in 1828 in McNairy County, Tennessee. In 1843, his family moved to Mississippi, and Lowrey served in the 2nd Mississippi Volunteers as a private during the Mexican War, though the regiment did not see combat. He became a Baptist minister and preached until the war began, at which point his congregation urged him to join the Confederacy. Lowrey served in the Mississippi militia until December 1861, when he was appointed colonel of the 4th Mississippi. In early April 1862, he became the commander of the 32nd Mississippi, which he led at Shiloh. He then led the regiment through the war until after Chickamauga. After the former commander of the brigade resigned, Lowrey received his commission to brigadier general and took control of the brigade. He fought bravely at Tunnel Hill and Ringgold Gap.

Also attached to the division was a battalion of artillery under Major Thomas R. Hotchkiss. The battalion consisted of three batteries. Key's Arkansas Battery had four twelve-pounder howitzers, while Swett's Mississippi Battery had four ten-pounder Parrott rifles and Semple's Alabama Battery fielded four twelve-pounder Napoleon smoothbores.[38] Cleburne's Division mustered 5,218 enlisted men on the firing line in the ranks and 540 officers at the beginning of the campaign for a total of 5,758. This does not include enlisted men detailed for non-combat duties or the artillery battalion.[39]

On the Sabbath, the Confederate leaders attended services with their men. General Johnston worshiped alongside corps commander Hood in a service led by General Polk, who was also Bishop of the Episcopal Diocese of Louisiana. They would need all the help they could get—divine or otherwise. But just in case, Johnston that day ordered Wheeler to take as much of his cavalry stationed upstream as he could spare and cross over the river, at which point he was to move behind the Federal lines, find out where they were going and cause as much destruction as he could if the opportunity arose. That night, Wheeler took most of his command over the river. The next day, Monday, May 23, the campaign renewed in earnest.[40]

Chapter 4

Crossing the Etowah

As the pre-dawn grey melted away with the rising sun, Monday, May 23, promised to be another clear and warm day. The hills and valleys along the Etowah River buzzed with Union activity. Even before the night sky began to lighten, officers and their orderlies were awake. Horses carried staff officers back and forth issuing orders and instructions. Reverie was at four o'clock in the morning. Soldiers awoke, lit fires and started a breakfast, which usually consisted of bacon, bread or hardtack and coffee. Companies and regiments fell in for inspection, where they were then counted off for duty or asked if they needed to see the surgeon or steward for sick call. One officer too sick to serve was Samuel Beatty, and this necessitated a major command change in the division. Beatty stepped down that morning, and Colonel Knefler took over the Third Brigade.

General George H. Thomas had dictated the line of march for his army's three corps in an order issued the night before. General Hooker's Twentieth Corps, which was to be on the road at 4:00 a.m., would march south from Cassville and cross the Etowah at Gillem's Bridge, camping below the river along Euharlee Creek. Howard's Fourth Corps would follow in their footsteps beginning at 8:00 a.m. Thomas ordered the First Division of the Cavalry Corps to begin its march at 4:00 a.m.; move west to Island Ford a few miles downstream, where they would cross the river; and then swing ahead and be in position ahead of the Twentieth Corps by nightfall. He also ordered the two divisions present from Major General John M. Palmer's Fourteenth Corps to cross at Island Ford and camp for the night behind the Fourth. A third division was stationed much farther west at Rome, Georgia, and would travel on its own toward Dallas. In addition to marching orders, Thomas issued instructions preventing straggling from the ranks, entering civilian dwellings, taking civilian property and the burning of buildings. As far as the other armies were concerned, the Army of the Tennessee would move over the river farther to the west and the Army of the Ohio to the east.[41]

Even today, with the aid of modern technology, moving an army of 100,000 men and their equipment is no easy task. Not surprisingly, things did not go according to plan. Thomas changed the line of march for the Twentieth Corps early in the morning. To the east of Gillem's Bridge stood Milam's Bridgehat—that is, until two days ago, when the Confederate cavalry burned it. However, there was still a good ford at that location, and Thomas diverted Hooker there. It didn't help that Howard's men got a late start, not leaving their camps until noon. But when the men of Wood's division filed out and began their march, they found the way blocked by Hooker's men. They wouldn't be able to resume the march until one o'clock.[42] When they did, most found the march hot and unpleasant, and some let the heat get the better of their tempers. Years later, the veterans of the 6th Indiana remembered how Andrew Sands of Company K vented the heat by "cursing everybody from the colonel up to the president." Otherwise, the walk to the river was uneventful.

Howard's men arrived at Gillem's Bridge at about five o'clock. They found the bridge burnt but still intact—the Confederates had apparently tried to burn the bridge but were unsuccessful. After crossing over, the men continued marching south past the small village of Euharlee before making camp at nightfall along Euharlee Creek at Barrett's Mill. This area of Georgia was relatively untouched by the war. Marcus Woodcock thought it was "an exceedingly beautiful and productive country, though but little of it was under cultivation at the time," while another soldier thought it "some of the finest country we had yet seen. It bore few marks of the bloody and ruinous struggle which was being waged elsewhere, yet it was now destined to receive its full share of the blighting curse which must fall alike upon all Rebellious soil." The officers of the 15th Ohio didn't organize regular foraging parties, so Thomas' directive notwithstanding, some of the men of the regiment "liberated" some local pigs and added fresh pork to the rations that night. Up ahead and now in front, Brigadier General Edward M. McCook's First Cavalry division spread out to cover the approaches to the army. They soon made contact with Confederate cavalry at Stilesborough.[43]

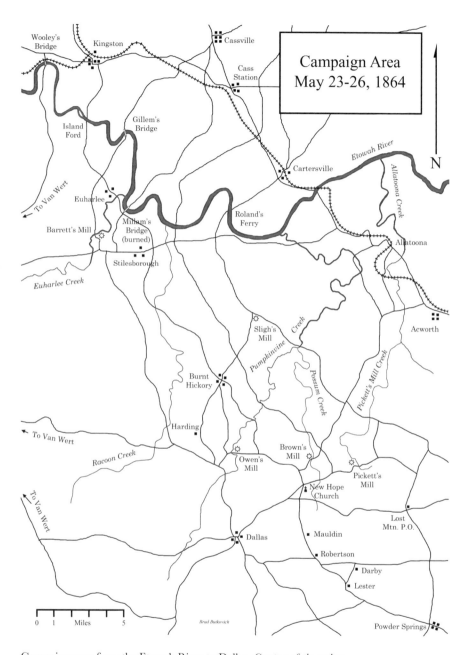

Campaign map from the Etowah River to Dallas. *Courtesy of the author.*

Thomas's change not only delayed the Fourth Corps but also General Schofield and his Twenty-Third Corps, the single corps composing the Army of the Ohio. When Hooker's men reached the crossing at Milam's Bridge, they found two pontoon bridges already spanning the river. That was very opportune for Hooker, who promptly marched his corps across, but rather inconvenient for Schofield, as Sherman had assigned to him for crossing. Now Hooker was in the way. Graciously, Schofield allowed Hooker's men to continue without raising a fuss, but he did send Sherman a note explaining the delay. This surprised Sherman, as he had expected Schofield to cross farther to the east and was unaware that Schofield had constructed the bridges at Milam's. The Twenty-Third Corps wouldn't be able to cross until the next day.[44]

Among those waiting to cross was William Price. He had marched from Cartersville to the Etowah "through very fine country that spread out in waving wheat fields as far as the eye could reach, promising a golden and abundant harvest." His regiment, the 6th East Tennessee, camped for the night in a beautiful grove next to a fine mansion whose owner had fled. The other regiments of the brigade, the 3rd East Tennessee, 80th Indiana, 25th Michigan and 13th Kentucky, did likewise. The two Tennessee regiments of the brigade were composed of volunteers from pro-Union East Tennessee and were often referred to as East Tennessee regiments to distinguish them from their Confederate counterparts. With the exception of the 80th Indiana, which fought at Perryville, the rest of the brigade had not seen much combat. Their combat experience so far had been chasing cavalry raiders in Kentucky and the minor East Tennessee/Knoxville campaign in the fall of 1863. The brigade was the First Brigade of the Second Division, Twenty-Third Corps, and was commanded by Brigadier General Nathaniel C. McLean.[45]

McLean, a forty-nine-year-old Harvard College graduate from Warren County, Ohio, was a lawyer before the war. When the rebellion began, he raised and organized the 75th Ohio and commissioned its colonel. He led the regiment in the early campaigns in the Shenandoah Valley in 1862. After the Battle of Cross Keys, he took command of his brigade. In August, at the Second Battle of Bull Run, he took up a position on Chinn Ridge, where he was to guard against any flank attack from the Confederates. When the enemy did attack, McLean and his outnumbered brigade fought valiantly, allowing the units behind him to rally and organize an effective defense. McLean earned his first star as a result. Unfortunately, Bull Run would be the apex of his career. At Chancellorsville in May 1863, McLean's brigade was part of Howard's Eleventh Corps and posted at the far end of the Union line. When Stonewall Jackson's famous flank attack struck the Union line, they struck McLean's men from the right and from behind. McLean tried to face his regiments in the right direction, but the size and ferocity of the attack prevented any successful defense. Howard, who refused to accept responsibility for the disposition and fate of his corps, kept his command. McLean, on the other hand, applied to be relieved of his command. Washington ordered him west to the Department of the Ohio, where he served as the department's provost marshal before taking to the field with a new brigade. It was his second chance at a field command.[46]

While the Twenty-Third Corps marked time and the Fourth Corps crossed at Gillem's Bridge, the Fourteenth Corps made its way toward Island Ford farther west. The journey was just as hot as it was for the Fourth. Dust from thousands of pounding feet rose through the air, permeating clothes and food and choking the breath from the lungs. It was almost impossible to see from one end of a regiment to another along the road, and the heat took its toll on some of them. In a Wisconsin regiment, undoubtedly one case of many that afternoon, a soldier fell with heatstroke. Luckily, an ambulance was following the regiment, and his comrades put him on board. He survived, but it would be a week before he could return to duty. Such a recovery was probably typical.[47]

Once they arrived at the river, the soldiers faced the prospect of having to cross it. Some of them opted to remove their shoes and socks (and some their underwear and pants as well) before crossing. They attached their bayonets to their rifles and hung the clothes. Others opted to wade in fully clothed. At least some removed their socks but put their shoes back on their bare feet. Their foresight became evident to those who remained barefoot, as rocks, both large and small, coated with years of slime covered the river bottom. Many a soldier disappeared under the current, only to resurface moments later thoroughly soaked. They either laughed or cursed their fortune, as did their comrades. But watch out! The one who laughed at his friend's misfortune was just as apt to be the next one under! It was a lighthearted moment on an otherwise hot and miserable day.[48] The experience of Corporal Ira S. Owens of the 74th Ohio was common:

> *Some of the boys prepared to wade by taking off their shoes and pantaloons. Others went right in, without taking off anything. I did so myself. When about halfway across, where the water was nearly breast deep and running very swift, I thought I would go ahead of some who were ahead of me,*

The Union Fourth Corps crossed the Etowah River on Gillem's Bridge at this spot. This bridge is a postwar structure. *Author's collection.*

when I stumbled and fell, losing my gun, and getting a complete wetting, filling my haversack with water and soaking my hardtack. I recovered my gun, which would not have been of much use should we have had occasion to use it.

It was a ludicrous sight to see the Seventy-fourth wading the river. If some artist had been present and sketched the scene, it would have made a laughable picture for some of our pictorials. One man of our regiment thought he would not wade the river but mounted on behind one of the boys, who was riding a mule. When about halfway across, the mule stumbled and fell, throwing them both over his head, completely ducking them. When we got over to the other side, the dust was all washed off.

We stayed an hour or so, and by the time we started again we were dry, it being very hot. After all, it was an advantage to us, for we were relieved of the dust, and the bathing caused us to feel very much refreshed.[49] *The last few yards of the crossing were the most dangerous. The opposite bank was higher than the riverbed, and the only way to ascent it was over a large felled tree that connected to a small island in the river. The current in the 40 yards from the island to the river was much swifter. Most of those climbing up the tree did so with ease, but at least one man fell and the current swept him away, never to be seen again.*[50]

Corporal Owens's 74th Ohio had a lot of company on its journey across the river, as there were five other regiments in his brigade: the 37th and 38th Indiana, 21st Ohio, 78th Pennsylvania and 1st Wisconsin. Together they constituted the Third Brigade, First Division, Fourteenth Army Corps in the Army of the Cumberland. Like most of the brigades in the army, they had seen their share of ups and downs during the war, and like most of the brigades in the Army of the Cumberland, it was a product of the brigade consolidations the previous fall. A few of the regiments had fought hard at Perryville, and all saw action at Stone's River. Half of the regiments in the brigade routed from the field at Chickamauga with their previous division, but those in the other half saw little or no combat. The standout was the 21st Ohio, which secured its fame on the second day by standing its ground during Thomas's stand at Horseshoe Ridge. Armed with Colt Revolving Rifles at the time, the men fought for six hours, sometimes repulsing entire brigades singlehandedly. But they had seen no real combat since then. They had remained behind to man the fortifications around Chattanooga during the assault on Missionary Ridge, and so far had made no real attacks during the current campaign. The brigade marched from Chattanooga with a total of 3,094 officers and men present for duty, with probably 2,887 or so available on the firing line.[51]

Leading the Third Brigade was Colonel Benjamin F. Scribner. Born in 1825, Scribner displayed an early interest in the military when he joined a local militia unit, the Spencer Grays. When war broke out with Mexico in 1846, the Grays offered their service to the governor of Indiana, becoming a company in the 2nd Indiana Volunteer Regiment. Scribner saw combat for the first time at Buena Vista. After the war, he wrote a small book about his experiences titled *Camp Life of a Volunteer, by One Who Saw the Elephant.* A successful druggist before the war, when hostilities broke out, he worried about how the conflict would affect his family if he volunteered. Conversations with Indiana governor Oliver P. Morton mollified him, and he soon became colonel of a militia regiment. Shortly afterward, the governor appointed him colonel of the 38th Indiana. His first major battle was Perryville, and he was elevated to command the brigade after his superior officer became ill. His command was handled roughly at Stone's River, and at Chickamauga, his brigade was routed from the field on the first day but fought well the second day until withdrawal at nightfall. With the reorganization of the army in October, he reverted to command of the 38th but rose again to brigade command when the 38th transferred to the Third Brigade and its brigadier was relieved for duty in Washington, D.C.[52]

The other officers of the division were all seasoned, capable veterans. The commander of the First Brigade was Brigadier General William P. Carlin, a career army officer. Carlin fought early in the war in Missouri and had served capably as a brigade commander since Perryville. He could be difficult to work with and was often at odds with his previous commanding officer, but he was a professional soldier through and through. His current brigade consisted of the 104th Illinois; 42nd and 88th Indiana; 15th Kentucky; 2nd, 33rd and 94th Ohio; and the 10th and 21st Wisconsin.

The Second Brigade commander was Brigadier General John H. King, another career officer. Almost trapped in Texas and forced to surrender at the very beginning of the war, he had risen through the ranks of the Regular Army before taking a brigadier general's commission before Chickamauga. He led a brigade of Regular Army troops, the only one in the Army of the Cumberland. At the beginning of the war, the Regulars provided a core of seasoned, professional soldiers, many of them having served in the numerous frontier posts before the war. However, three years of conflict had seriously depleted their ranks, and replacements had to be trained from scratch, just like any other new recruits. In addition, the volunteer regiments had three years of combat experience under their belt and were now just as proficient as the Regulars. Still, the strict discipline and *esprit de corps* of the Regulars were high, and they still considered themselves an elite unit. As a result of the brigade mergers of the previous fall, there were now a few volunteer regiments in the brigade, which was composed of the 1st and 2nd Battalions of the 15th Infantry, the 1st and 2nd Battalions of the 16th Infantry, the 1st and 2nd Battalions of the 18th Infantry, the 1st Battalion of the 19th Infantry, the 11th Michigan and the 69th Ohio.[53]

Brigadier General Richard W. Johnson commanded the First Division, Fourteenth Corps. Yet another career officer, the thirty-seven-year-old had, like King, escaped from Texas without surrendering when that state seceded. Commanding cavalry during the first year of the war, he ran afoul of legendary Confederate raider John Hunt Morgan, who captured him in late summer 1862. Soon exchanged, he took command of an infantry division before Stone's River and had held a division command since. With the exception of the assault on Missionary Ridge, he had never won an

Brigadier General Richard W. Johnson. *Courtesy of Library of Congress.*

offensive victory, and even there, a feeble Rebel counterattack almost routed his division back down the slope. In fact, except for a few regiments at Shiloh, the men in his division also lacked an offensive victory during the war, except Missionary Ridge. Perryville and Stone's River were defensive victories, but Chickamauga was a defeat. Confederate counterattacks during these battles overturned whatever tactical advances the troops made. The 8,693 officers and men who marched from Chattanooga were veterans to be sure, but they needed firm, aggressive leadership to bring about an offensive victory. Only time would tell if the men of the First Division would get that leadership, as they went into camp along Euharlee Creek that evening.[54]

The last thing the men did before going to sleep that night was to build entrenchments to protect their camp and the army's line of battle from enemy attack. While trenches and breastworks had been used extensively by the two armies since Chattanooga the previous fall, it had now become standard practice to build fortifications each night. First, the men gathered wood in the form of fence rails (those not used to make camp fires), old logs, newly felled trees and, if necessary, boards from houses. These were stacked in a line and often held in place by vertical stakes. The men then dug a ditch on the friendly side of the works and piled the dirt up against the logs on the outside. The ditch was deep enough so that a person could stand in it with only his head and shoulders showing above the log, giving him just enough room to shoot. For longer stays, the men dug the ditch even deeper, leaving a step called a parapet for the men to shoot from. Then, they placed another log called a "head log" on top of the vertical stakes, leaving enough room to shoot between the top of the works and the head log. This provided some additional protection to the head and upper body. If time allowed, they added an additional ditch on the outside of the works, and that dirt added to the pile. From Chattanooga to Atlanta, the Georgia countryside would be scarred with trenches at least every fifteen miles or so, and the same would be true in Virginia from the Rapidan to Petersburg.

All this Federal activity did not go unnoticed south of the river, as the Confederate cavalry reported the movement just after dawn. Brigadier General Lawrence Sullivan "Sul" Ross's cavalry brigade reported Hooker's crossing on the pontoons at Milam's Bridge first thing in the morning. In fact, it was Ross's cavalry and those of his parent division that McCook encountered at Stilesborough. Wheeler also sent word from north of the river gathered from prisoners and citizens during the night on the movements of the Federal armies. Johnston was no fool, and he had three days to read the same map that Sherman did. Now that he knew the river crossings east of Allatoona were safe, he promptly issued orders putting the army in motion toward Dallas. Hardee issued the orders for his corps to move at 8:30 a.m., so given the time it takes to draft orders and deliver them, Johnston probably made his decision between 7:00 and 7:30 a.m. Even before the Union Fourth Corps was on the road, the Confederate army was on the move to intercept them![55]

Cleburne's Division moved out toward Dallas at 10:00 a.m. Lucius Polk's Brigade led the way, followed by Govan, Granbury, Lowrey and the artillery. Walker's Division got on the road at 10:30 a.m., followed by Major General William B. Bate's division at 11:00 a.m. and Major General Benjamin F. Cheatham's division as soon as Bate's had cleared. Johnston likewise ordered Polk's Corps toward Dallas, but on another road farther south to avoid congestion. Hood's Corps remained at Allatoona for the time being.[56]

As Captain Foster marched, he broke in a new pair of shoes he had received the night before. Unfortunately, they were too big, and no smaller size was available. The day was just as hot and dusty for him and his fellow Confederates as it was for their adversaries to the north, but the march seemed to have come off without incident. The columns stopped about 4:00 p.m. and made camp. A light rain fell, enough to cool them off and lay down the dust. A few Confederate sources noted the rain, but none in the Union. It's possible that it was a typical localized Georgia spring shower and that it didn't rain near Euharlee that evening.[57]

Hardee issued orders at 10:00 p.m. that night detailing the next day's march—it would be an early start. Bate's Division would begin at 2:00 a.m. and stop at New Hope Church, a small church that also lent its name to the crossroads where it was located. From there, the division brigades would picket the roads west and to the north, reinforcing the Confederate cavalry. Cleburne's Division would start at 3:00 a.m., pass Bate at New Hope Church and turn south on the road toward Atlanta. Walker was to follow an hour later and Cheatham an hour after Walker. Once the corps had passed, Bate would recall his division and bring up the rear. Their objective was to take up a blocking position along the main road from Atlanta to Dallas.[58]

The first day of the renewed campaign had been a series of hits and misses for both sides. For the Union, a misunderstanding about where each unit would cross led to a change of orders that left an entire corps trapped on the north side of the river for a day. Otherwise, everything had gone according to plan. The Armies of the Cumberland and the Tennessee were both across the river. Thomas's Fourth, Fourteenth and Twentieth Corps were in position along Euharlee Creek, screened by McCook's cavalry.

McPherson's army had crossed at Wooley's Bridge and was on the way to Van Wert. The day had also gone well for Johnston, at least on the surface. His cavalry had notified him immediately of the crossings, and he responded quickly, putting two-thirds of his army in motion before some of the Union soldiers had left their campsites. However, this doesn't excuse the fact that the Federals were able to cross the river at all. Johnston had done nothing to dispute the crossings in force and had failed to burn Gillem's and Woolley's Bridges. Nor did Johnston head straight toward the enemy columns in an attempt to attack them while they were advancing, as Robert E. Lee had done against Grant in the Wilderness earlier that month. By following the road directly from Allatoona to Euharlee instead of heading toward Dallas, Hardee's Corps, with Polk's behind him, could have ended the day near Stilesborough and in a position to strike Thomas the next morning. Instead, Johnston opted to get ahead of them and block them. These failures, while subtle, are important. By failing to explore or implement these options, Johnston lost two opportunities to offset Sherman's numerical superiority. The next day promised to be another long, hot day of marching as the two forces moved into position.

Chapter 5

Through the Pine Barrens

George Thomas also issued orders on the evening of the twenty-third for the next day's march. McCook's cavalry would lead the advance to Burnt Hickory, while one division of the Twentieth Corps would head east to Raccoon Creek to act as a blocking force in case any Confederates appeared from that direction. The rest of the corps were to march through Stilesborough and then south to Burnt Hickory. The Fourth Corps was to follow the Twentieth, and the Fourteenth Corps would bring up the rear and follow behind the Fourth. Schofield's Army of the Ohio would cross over the pontoons at Milam's Bridge and relieve the Twentieth Corps division at Raccoon Creek, allowing that division to march south and reunite with its corps.[59]

Reveille sounded at 3:30 a.m., and it began to get light at 5:00 a.m. The sun broke above the horizon, filtering through the surrounding forests at about 5:30 a.m. The pickets from Wood's division were recalled to camp at 6:00 a.m. It would be a long day for those on outpost duty, as they marched all day, stood guard all night and would have to march all day again. One godsend to help keep them awake was coffee, a staple in the Union army. Each day at daybreak (and while on the march if the soldiers thought they had enough time), the soldiers started their fires. The men crushed the coffee, which was issued roasted but whole bean, in a quart pail using the socket end of a bayonet like a pestle. According to Brigadier General Jacob D. Cox, "At break of day, every camp was musical with the clangor of these primitive coffee-mills." Breakfast followed soon after.[60]

Hooker's corps, of course, was up earlier and was on the road at daylight. The men of Howard's corps began their march at 7:00 a.m. Wood's division led the way, followed by Newton and Stanley. It was another hot day. The roads were those in name only. In reality, they were mere paths through the forest. There were a few small settlements and farms along the way, and by about 1:00 p.m., the corps reached the banks of Raccoon Creek. There the men ran up against the wagon trains and artillery of Hooker's corps, so they halted for lunch. The distant rumble of artillery up ahead, most likely exchanges between the cavalry screening the two armies, reminded them that the enemy was still nearby.[61]

The men of the 15th Ohio spread out in a large field near the creek and found a large quantity of tobacco, a precious southern commodity. Colonel Gibson found out about it and ordered it distributed among the rest of the brigade. Soon the men with pipes were enjoying a refreshing smoke, and those without fashioned new ones from corn cobs. Undoubtedly, coffee was also enjoyed by all. The cool waters of the creek were also an inviting site to many, and the stream soon filled with men washing and cooling themselves off. Officers rode their horses into the creek, and soon "dog-robbers," as one artilleryman put it, were washing the horses. One general asked a soldier washing his feet nearby to fill up the officer's cup with water for a drink. The man hesitated, telling the general it probably wasn't safe to drink with everyone washing upstream. "Oh, never mind that—I've drank worse," replied the general good-naturedly as he drank two cups.[62]

After two hours, the march resumed. The countryside between Raccoon Creek and Dallas was a wilderness of ravines and hills, a southwest extension of the Allatoona Mountains. The forests themselves were barren, with endless stands of yellow pines. But some of the men still took in the beauty of their surroundings. Others, like Lieutenant Woodcock, noted how he had seen few citizens along the way. So great was their isolation that the ones he did encounter didn't know where the Confederates were and seemed to hardly know there was a war on at all. This had also been gold country before the great California Gold Rush, and from time to time, soldiers would pick up beautiful specimens of gold bearing crystallized quartz. Inevitably, the rocks would return to the country and roadside from which they came, as the soldiers gave more importance to lightening their load in the here and now and less to the thought of riches in a future they may never see.[63]

The Fourth Corps made it to Burnt Hickory around 5:30 p.m., depending on where one was in the column, having walked about ten miles. While marching from Raccoon Creek, the skies steadily grew more overcast, and by the time the men reached their bivouac, a storm was brewing. Shortly after making camp, the storm broke. But by that time, most were safe and dry in their shelter tents. Unfortunately, that didn't include the commissary men issuing beef around the camp. They were soon soaked to the skin, as were any teamsters, artillerymen and infantry still marching to catch up.[64]

Those marching to catch up included the men of Palmer's Fourteenth Corps. Following Howard, they had much the same experience during the march, but there were many more stops and starts since they were the last in line. Johnson had his division on the road at 10:00 a.m. only to find that he had to repair the bridge over Euharlee Creek in order to get his artillery across. Two miles out from there, his men had to wait for Stanley's division of the Fourth Corps to clear the road before they could continue.[65] Along the way, Captain Henry Ottos and his men in the 104th Illinois found out that the Rebs weren't the only enemies to look out for. In a humorous account, he wrote:

> *The following day we ran against an enemy on which we had not calculated. He was not the least scared by our rifles and batteries and besides he made us "Git" quick. Our Regt. happened to be in advance. Near the narrow road lay a half rotten small brush pile. I do not know whether some of the boys had disturbed the pile but this I know that a colony of yellow jackets or wasps had their domicile in there and they claimed exclusive right of way. They got it to without much dispute. It did not take a minute and the whole Regt. was whisking through the underbrush trying to lose them, made a considerable flank movement.[66]*

By the time it was dark, it had already started to rain, and the head of the Fourteenth Corps had only reached Raccoon Creek. There the men of the corps assembled, built works and laid down for the night.[67]

Farther to the east, the Twenty-Third Corps dutifully crossed the Etowah early in the morning and relieved the division of the Twentieth Corps, allowing it to march south and rejoin Hooker. Continuing east, the Twenty-Third Corps turned south at the road leading from Roland's Ferry. Occasionally skirmishing with the enemy, the corps halted at Sligh's Mill for the night. Around nightfall, the Army of the Ohio's lone cavalry division, under Major General George Stoneman, arrived to take up the duties of leading and screening the infantry.[68]

What kept Stoneman's division north of the river for so long was Wheeler's cavalry. On the morning of the twenty-fourth, Wheeler rode with several cavalry brigades north from their camps along the north bank of the Etowah, captured a wagon supply train and advanced to Cass Station. There the retreating Federals burned even more supplies to keep them out of Rebel hands. Stoneman counterattacked but failed to drive Wheeler off. Still, enough Federal infantry support nearby prevented Wheeler from doing any more damage, and he withdrew south to the river. Leaving the safety of the rail line to the infantry, Stoneman was now free to rejoin Schofield. He turned south and caught up with the advanced units of the Army of the Ohio at Sligh's Mill. On the extreme Union right, Brigadier General Kenner Garrard's Second Cavalry Division, leading McPherson's Army of the Tennessee, camped for the night on Pumpkinvine Creek between Van Wert and Dallas. The balance of the Army of Tennessee itself was still at Van Wert.[69]

The Confederates too had a long day marching. For Cleburne's men, it was mostly uneventful. They began on time at 3:00 a.m. after receiving two days worth of corn bread and bacon. The men in Captain Foster's company passed the time speculating on their destination. Some guessed at Florida, while others put forward Cuba (via a pontoon bridge) as the ultimate objective. Others dismissed this out of hand, as the Yanks could easily put a torpedo (mine) under the bridge and demolish it. One can only smile and imagine these types of tongue-in-cheek conversations the common soldier bantered about to relieve the boredom of trudging down a never-ending dusty road. But end the road did, at least for the day. The division reached the Robertson house on the Atlanta Road, but due to a lack of enough water in the area needed to support the number of troops present, General Hardee ordered the corps to continue five miles farther southeast to the village of Powder Springs. This is a great example of how logistics, not tactics, can often influence the shape and creation of a battle. Cleburne's Division arrived at Powder Springs about 2:00 p.m., though not all of them camped at the village.[70]

On the way to Powder Springs, Private Smith in his wagon enjoyed a luxury not usually enjoyed by his fellow Confederates: fresh milk. He described the day itself as "very hot," and the canteen of milk given to him by his friend and wagonmate Robert was undoubtedly a refreshing change from his normal canteen full of water. Smith described Powder Springs as "two churches, just across the road from each other, a dwelling house and a graveyard at our camp." He and a few others were lucky enough to appropriate one of the churches as shelter for the night. Smith and Robert put together two benches for a bed. Come evening, the same hard rain that swamped the Union troops to the north fell on the Confederates. Somebody got some candles and a chaplain, and they decided to hold church services that night. Members of Cleburne's staff, who were also in the church, threatened to kick them all out, arguing that they needed their sleep. Fortunately (or unfortunately, depending on your point of view), the staffers were called away into the rain to meet with the division commander. The service continued, and the chaplain stayed to eat supper with the men.[71]

To be fair to the staff, they undoubtedly had a busy day during which they wrote and delivered dozens of orders. Paperwork had to be completed, and they carried out routine errands and sometimes reconnaissance. They spent most of the day on horseback going here or there. Now that Hardee's Corps was camped at Powder Springs, preparations for the next day's march began. Events to the northwest near Dallas dictated the course of action. Bate's Division, left behind to reinforce the cavalry screen near Dallas, had clashed during the day with the Garrard's cavalry advancing from Van Wert. Johnston's orders for the next day were for Hardee's Corps to move toward Dallas, much of it reversing course and going back on the same road on which they marched into Powder Springs. The other two Confederate Corps had also been in motion during the day. Polk's Corps had paralleled Hardee's march south on roads farther east. His orders for the next day were to march to Dallas and deploy on Hardee's right. Back at Allatoona, thanks to Wheeler's foray, Johnston felt the pass was in no immediate danger, so he ordered Hood's Corps south to join the rest of the army. After marching all day, it ended on the twenty-fourth about four miles northeast of New Hope Church.[72]

May 24 had been another hot day marching on dry dusty roads, followed by a common Georgia spring thunderstorm. Sherman's armies had left the valley of the Etowah and plunged into the barren wilderness of the Allatoona Mountains. They were converging on Dallas from the north and west, but with the exception of a few clashes with Rebel cavalry and Bate's Division, they had no real idea where the Confederates were or how many of them there were. On the other hand, Johnston quickly found out where the Union columns were during the course of the day and had moved promptly to put his forces in a position to block their advance. A collision the next day was inevitable.

Chapter 6

Collision at New Hope Church

S herman crafted his orders for the next day to culminate in the concentration of his three armies at Dallas. McPherson was to continue his approach to Dallas from the west. Schofield was to march from Sligh's Mill to Burnt Hickory and then follow the Army of the Cumberland to Dallas. Thomas's task was a bit more complicated. The Twentieth Corps would split. One of its divisions would follow McCook's cavalry on one road, while the other two would take another. Howard's Fourth Corps would follow the two Twentieth Corps divisions or, if possible, move overland to the west and take yet another road heading in the direction of Dallas. The two divisions of the Fourteenth Corps would follow Howard. Thomas's hope was to converge on Dallas using a number of different roads to relieve the traffic congestion as much as possible in the dense forest.[73]

Reveille was at 4:00 a.m. for Wood's division, but Williams's division of the Twentieth Corps was already on the road in front of them. They did not start their march until 9:00 a.m. Newton's division was in the lead, followed by Stanley's half an hour later. Wood began his march at 10:00 a.m. In the 79th Indiana at least, new shoes were due to be issued that morning, and one man in each company was detailed to remain behind, collect the badly needed shoes and then catch up with their company and distribute them. It's possible that other regiments in their brigade or even the rest of the division experienced something similar. Once underway, the division accidently marched north for a little while but then corrected course and found the parallel road to the west. There they found that the other two divisions of the corps had already filled the road, so they had to mark time for about two hours until the route cleared.[74]

While marching through the wilderness, the 86th Indiana passed a solitary cabin along the way. The woman residing there remarked to the boys that they couldn't fool her—she knew Sherman was flanking again. When pressed, she explained that she knew Sherman was flanking because she had seen his "flanking machines" pass by on the road earlier. The men knew she was doubtlessly referring to a battery that was travelling ahead of them. Its cannon, attached to limbers and pulled by a team of six horses, along with ammunition caissons, likewise pulled by a similar team, for all the world looked like infernal machines to this country woman. Such sentiment amused the soldiers to no end, but they also realized that she wasn't far from the truth. The artillery—and, in fact, the whole army—was one large machine snaking its way through the wilderness toward a confrontation with the Rebels.[75]

That confrontation was not long in coming. After traveling several miles toward Dallas, the Twentieth Corps' Second Division, commanded by Brigadier General John W. Geary, came to an unmapped road heading off to the east. Hooker was with him at the head of the column, and the two conferred about the new road. The main road clearly continued on toward Dallas, but for some reason, Hooker decided to turn left. Perhaps he thought he could further relieve road congestion. Or maybe he thought it was a short cut. Whatever the reason, it turned out to be wrong. After crossing Pumpkinvine Creek at Owen's Mill, where Hooker had to use his mounted personal escort to secure the bridge, Geary ran into advanced elements of Hood's Corps.[76]

Hood had reached New Hope Church early in the day, at which point Johnston ordered him to halt and form along the crossroads facing northwest. The end result would be that Hardee would anchor the army's left at Dallas, Polk the middle and Hood the right. Hood deployed Major General Alexander P. Stewart's Division in the center astride the road to Owen's Mill, Major General Carter L. Stevenson's Division to Stewart's right and Major General Thomas C. Hindman's Division on Stewart's left. Notified that the Federals were near by the pickets Hooker had chased away at Pumpkinvine Creek, Hood ordered a regiment of infantry up the road in that direction to feel out the enemy. That regiment kicked up a beehive of activity as surely as Captain Ottos's company had by the roadside the previous day. The Confederate regiment attacked the Union skirmishers as soon as they made contact, and before long, each side was feeding in units as fast as they could. The Confederates were vastly outnumbered though, and several miles ahead of their main line. Having delayed Geary's division as long as they could, the Confederates, only in brigade strength, retired back to New Hope Church.[77]

Thomas was now at the front, too. He, Hooker and Geary agreed that such an aggressive delaying action, where the weak Confederate force had actually attacked several times, must be a sign that a larger force was to their front. They were correct. Hood's entire corps was up ahead at the crossroads. Fearing for the safety of the isolated division, Thomas ordered Hooker to have Geary entrench and sent messengers for reinforcements. Sherman, who was back at Owen's Mill, ordered Thomas to have Geary attack immediately, stating, "There haven't been twenty Rebels there today." Thomas, with a better grasp of the tactical situation than his superior, wisely demurred. To have sent Geary to attack Hood's whole entrenched corps would have been a disaster. The other two divisions of the corps arrived shortly. Now with his corps united, Hooker switched from the defensive to the offensive and deployed his corps to attack.[78]

Howard received Thomas's call for reinforcements at about 2:00 p.m. while at the Harding house, delivered by Lieutenant Colonel John Mendenhall. Howard immediately ordered the divisions of his corps to close up on the road, that is, for everybody to move forward and eliminate any gaps between the units that might have formed during the march. After marching a few hundred yards past the Harding house, they found a small country road, and the column turned left. Howard ordered General Wood, as the last division in the column, to guard the wagon supply trains and to leave detachments to watch the numerous road intersections they were to pass. It was a hard march over hills, hollows, bad roads and rough country.[79]

Newton's division, at the head of the column, arrived around 5:00 p.m. behind Hooker as the latter was just finishing the deployment of his corps. Thomas had Howard deploy Newton on the right side of the road and when Stanley arrived put him in behind Newton. Wood's division, having the road blocked by wagons and other traffic, did not arrive on the scene until after dark. Hooker began his advance at 5:30 p.m. and after traveling about a mile confronted Hood's corps behind their breastworks. Hooker's men charged repeatedly but were ultimately unable to carry the works, sustaining moderate losses. At about 6:30, Hooker sent word back for Howard to move forward and support him. Newton and Stanley began moving but found the off-road terrain too difficult to negotiate. They moved back to the left, got on the road and moved toward Hooker, although Stanley started about an hour and a half later because nobody could find him to deliver his orders.[80]

The sounds of the fighting carried far afield. Back with Wood's division, the men of the 15th Ohio heard firing "so continuous that we knew we had met the enemy in force." As the fighting intensified and the pitch of battle rose, the clouds began to darken and thunder rumbled in the distance. Suddenly,

> *in the midst of the din, there was one mighty peal of thunder so loud, so deep, so profound, that we were awe-stricken. It made our heavy guns sound like the snapping of matches in comparison. It was comforting as well as awe-inspiring, for it made us remember that God was on His throne and still watching over His world. No one who heard that peal of thunder could ever forget it.*[81]

Newton and Stanley arrived behind the Twentieth Corps at dusk. The march had been tough. Wounded soldiers heading toward the rear clogged the road to New Hope Church. The detritus of battle lay everywhere. When they arrived, Hooker asked Newton to deploy on the left of the road and extend his line to the east. Howard gave the order, and Newton's men plunged into the darkening woods to the left. However, they didn't finish forming up into line of battle on Hooker's left until it was night and therefore didn't take part in any of the fighting that evening. Stanley's men stayed by the roadside. At dusk, the skies opened, and torrents of rain fell on the living and the dead.[82]

Most of Wood's division didn't cross Pumpkinvine Creek at Owen's Mill until late in the evening. William Stahl claimed that he and the 49th Ohio of Gibson's First Brigade didn't cross until 6:30 p.m., while the men of the 79th Indiana in the Third Brigade crossed "at dark." Marcus Woodcock wrote:

> *Just enough rain had fallen to make the hard beaten road slippery, and we found great difficulty in ascending the hill from the creek. We then advanced by slow degrees a few miles farther, and after almost being wearied to death by continual standing, we were finally* [about 10:00 p.m.] *ordered to bivouac by the roadside in the order in which we had marched.*

The scene as the division trudged up the road in the rain toward the battlefield was a sorry spectacle. Wounded men from the fight lined the woods along the road, their pale faces visible in the fires that compassionate camp followers had lit for them. Long after dark, in the pouring rain, the men of Wood's division arrived behind Stanley.[83]

After seeing to the men of his division, Howard himself made his way back to a small church they had passed on the way up. There, under torches made from pine knots, the surgeons and their assistants tended to the wounded. With "sleeves rolled up, and hands and arms, clothes and faces sprinkled with blood," they did the best they could to treat the mangled and broken men brought to them. Up at the front, Hooker's men began digging in where they lay, stacking logs, digging trenches and keeping a steady fire upon the enemy to keep him occupied. The rain and the skirmishers kept up their respective work all night long.[84]

Back at Raccoon Creek, the Fourteenth Corps didn't move at all during the day. The men of the corps stayed in their camps as the supply trains of the Twentieth Corps moved past them. Some of the men went to work helping the wagons negotiate the crossing and moving up the banks and hills along the creek, which had been made slippery by the rains from the previous day. The Army of the Ohio didn't fare much better. They stayed in camp at Sligh's Mill under orders from Sherman to allow McPherson's Army of the Tennessee time to approach Dallas from the west. At 5:00 p.m., the corps finally began its march to Burnt Hickory but upon arriving there found the roads south clogged with wagons. Turning south, Schofield continued the march with Second and Third Divisions, leaving the First Division behind at Burnt Hickory to guard the supply trains. The road traffic, storms and darkness made it a miserable trek. Schofield rode ahead before nightfall to coordinate the movement of his army with Sherman. By midnight, the corps hadn't even reached Pumpkinvine Creek, and they halted to rest. Word came back that Schofield's horse had stumbled in the mud in the dark, throwing the general against a tree and badly bruising his leg. Schofield relinquished command of the corps, put General Cox in command and relayed the order to advance the two divisions and report to General Sherman for orders upon arrival. After an hour's rest, the men were on their feet again. They reached the area behind the Fourth Corps at daybreak. They may have gotten a late start, but the men of the Twenty-Third Corps made up for it with a grueling night march—and the promise of little sleep the next day. On the far right, the Army of the Tennessee had moved up from Van Wert and made camp along Pumpkinvine Creek for the night.[85]

As Hood was fighting Thomas at New Hope Church, Hardee's Corps was making its way toward Dallas. Cleburne's men were up by 1:00 a.m. and ready to march by 3:00. William Smith had the luxury of hot coffee—with sugar no less—but it is doubtful that many others were so lucky, as coffee was more of a northern staple. The division started its march at 3:00 a.m. The rain the previous night had softened the roads, making the journey a little more difficult for teamsters like Smith, but soon Cleburne's Division had retraced its steps to the house of Henry Lester. There it turned right and made its way northeast until it arrived at the home of George Darby at about 9:00 a.m., where it laid for the rest of the day. Cooks issued rations, and many of the men caught up on their sleep.[86]

The men camped at the Darby house clearly heard the cannons and musketry from the fight at New Hope Church. Cleburne was on the road again at dusk, and orders arrived from Hardee at about 10:30 p.m. Instead of continuing toward Dallas, Cleburne's Division was to head toward Hood. The orders were to march at 4:00 a.m., but the men were already on the road. Still, they weren't making very good progress. The thunderstorm drenching the fight at New Hope Church was also soaking them. In addition, Walker's men were in front of them, and troops from Polk's Corps were already at their ultimate destination, the Maulding house (also spelled Maldin, Mauldin and Malden in various sources) on the road north of the Robertson house. Cleburne halted his men where they were and sought clarification from Hardee. Hardee replied that they were to camp where they were and start marching again at 4:00 a.m. as ordered, probably with the hope that the route would be clear by then. The men had been standing in the road for a good thirty minutes while this back-and-forth was going on and were grateful for the orders to fall out. Wet clothes made it difficult to get comfortable, and soon the men had torn down all the fences lining the right-of-way, undoubtedly to the consternation of their owners, and fires sprang up along the roadside.[87]

By the night of the twenty-fifth, the battle lines were beginning to take shape. McPherson's Army of the Tennessee was approaching Dallas from the west. Bate's and Cheatham's Divisions were near the town, and the rest of Hardee's Corps was south of New Hope Church near the Robertson house, where they could block McPherson's further advance or reinforce Hood. Hood was at New Hope Church, blocking the Army of the Cumberland and the Army of the Ohio from marching further south. During the night, Polk's Corps made its way into position on Hood's left, extending the line toward Dallas. Johnston had succeeded in stopping Sherman cold in his swing around Allatoona. Now it was up to each of them to see who could gain an advantage over the other in the tangled wilderness of Paulding County.

Chapter 7

Moving to the Right

A s soon as the sky brightened enough with the coming dawn for men to discern each other in the forest, the desultory "pop pop pop" of individual muskets along the lines at New Hope Church melded into a low, steady roar. At the road from New Hope Church to Owen's Mill, the lines were only eighty-five yards apart. Wagons brought more tools to the front, and Hooker's men dug deeper into the earth. If the two lines were very close, the men merely fired away at the opposing trench through the gap below the head log, often without even bothering to aim. If there was enough distance between the two lines, regiments deployed skirmishers into that no man's land. There they took cover behind whatever was available. Each man also dug a hole of his own for shelter called a rifle pit, which is the modern equivalent of a foxhole. Some sharpshooters climbed trees, often farther back from the lines but with a clear field of fire to the enemy works. From there they did their best to keep the enemy pinned down. On the twenty-sixth, Union skirmishers and sharpshooters did a particularly good job of preventing Confederate artillerymen from effectively manning their batteries.[88]

Howard's Fourth Corps behind and to the left of Hooker sprang into action early. Newton's division had moved up on Hooker's left during the night, but the darkness had prevented them from forming in an orderly fashion and establishing the best tactical position. A small gap existed between Newton's right and Geary's left, leading the commander of Hooker's leftmost division to believe that there were no troops there. Newton's men also hadn't entrenched during the night. As soon as it was light, the brigades of the division sent out their skirmishers to push back their Confederate counterparts as much as possible and then adjusted their lines to take best advantage of the terrain. Brigadier General Nathan Kimball's brigade deployed on the right, adjacent to Geary. The brigade of Brigadier General George D. Wagner was in the center, while Brigadier General Charles G. Harker's brigade constituted the end of the line on the left. Once the regiments were all on line and in position, they too began digging in. Howard also ordered General Stanley, whose division at the moment was located behind Newton, to fill the gap between Kimball and Geary with a few regiments from his division.[89]

The brigade bugler for Colonel Gibson sounded reveille a little before 3:00 a.m., but the colonel quickly told him to stop. Other regimental buglers were also cautioned not to play. Instead, officers and non-commissioned officers (NCOs) went along the lines and woke up the men. Soon the rest of Wood's division was awake. The men prepared their breakfasts, and an hour later, orders passed along the line to move out. General Howard ordered Wood's division to move to the left of Newton and extend the line farther east. The Dallas–Acworth Road intersected the road between Owen's Mill and New Hope Church behind the Union line. Angling northeast, it provided an easy avenue for reaching the flank of the army. Behind and to the left of Harker, who was oriented south, was a hill, and Wood deployed his division on its crest facing east. This was a precaution in case the Confederates launched an attack against the exposed Union line at dawn. Gibson's brigade connected with Harker at a right angle, and Hazen's men fell in on Gibson's left. Knefler's brigade remained behind in reserve. Once in position, the frontline brigades began digging in.[90]

The new line was near the western edge of a large field. In the middle of the field was a house, which the family still occupied. The Union skirmishers were on the western edge, while their Confederate opponents, probably from Stevenson's Division, were on the other side. The 32nd Indiana drew skirmish duty for Gibson's brigade that morning. To the east at the bottom of the hill was Possum Creek, which flowed almost vertically north to south. The Dallas–Acworth Road crossed the creek at Brown's Mill a few hundred yards northeast of Hazen's position. At first, General Wood admonished his men not to bother entrenching, as he expected an order to advance at any moment. And indeed, he issued the order to advance soon afterward. However, the Rebel skirmish line proved stronger than anticipated, and the 32nd Indiana couldn't make any headway across the field. The rest of the brigade went back to digging.[91]

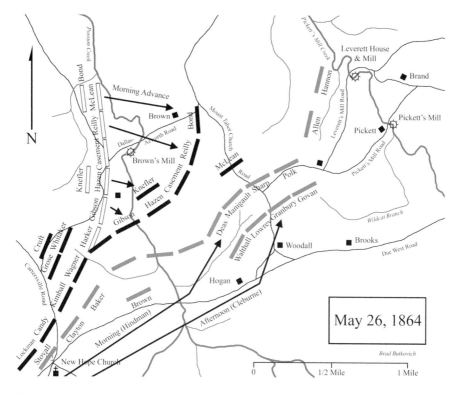

Operations as the Union Army crosses Possum Creek and covers Mount Tabor Church Road. *Courtesy of the author.*

Several hours passed, and according to First Lieutenant Alexis Cope, the adjutant of the 15th Ohio, the entire chain of command visited the line, including Wood, Howard, Thomas and Sherman himself. At about 8:00 a.m., the Twenty-Third Corps arrived and formed on Wood's left, opposite Brown's Mill. The two brigades of General Cox's Third Division connected to Hazen, while the two brigades of Brigadier General Milo S. Hascall formed the extreme left. Hascall's two brigades formed with a one-brigade front, one behind the other. General McLean's First Brigade was in front, and Colonel John R. Bond's Second Brigade was directly behind in support. Bond's brigade consisted of the 107th Illinois, 23rd Michigan and 45th, 111th and 118th Ohio regiments.[92]

Dinner was issued to the men of the 15th Ohio (lunch was more often referred to as dinner in the nineteenth century), but the men had only a few minutes to quickly swallow the meal before the order passed along the line to advance again. At about 9:00 a.m., the two brigades of the division advanced across the field under the watchful eyes of the commanding generals. Knefler followed in support. The Twenty-Third Corps advanced on the left. This time, the Confederates gave way with little opposition. As Wood's division advanced, it wheeled to the right. Gibson's brigade kept in contact with Harker on the right, and the entire division pivoted like a gate. The 32nd Indiana and Hazen's skirmishers led the way. Splashing across Possum Creek, which wasn't very deep, the Federal skirmishers forced the Confederates back up the low heights on the opposite side. Once Gibson was facing south on line with Harker, the left of his brigade rested on the creek. Hazen's brigade moved up on the left and took control of high ground on the west side of the creek. Possum Creek may not have been much of a barrier, but the banks prevented wagons and artillery from crossing anywhere except at a ford. Pioneers rapidly constructed a bridge behind the new line, and soon the 6th Ohio Battery rumbled across and went into position on the hill with Hazen. The added firepower forced the Confederate skirmishers to withdraw further, and Hazen was able to move forward to link up with Gibson, his right resting on the creek.[93]

The new position faced another large field, about three hundred yards across, and on the opposite side was the main Confederate line. The hill the division had previously occupied that morning was an ideal spot for artillery, and before long, two batteries crowned the rise facing south. Soon the Union and Confederate batteries were dueling, and they would continue sporadically throughout the day. Even General Howard took the time to sight in a cannon, possibly from the 6th Ohio, and fire it at the Rebels. Gibson and Hazen's men spent the rest of the afternoon and evening building earthworks at their new location. During the evening, the 15th Wisconsin and half of the 15th Ohio relieved the hardworking 32nd Indiana on the brigade skirmish line, giving the latter a much-deserved rest.[94]

The Twenty-Third Corps advanced on Wood's left, but instead of wheeling like a hinge, they kept a more easterly facing to protect the army's flank. After crossing Possum Creek, Cox's division connected with Hazen's brigade but faced more to the southeast, curving north. Hascall's division continued almost due east along the Dallas–Acworth Road, passing the sawmill and the Brown cabin. They took up a position just west of the intersection of Dallas–Acworth Road and Mount Tabor Church Road, about a half-mile east of the mill. The brigades faced due east.[95]

In the afternoon, McLean's brigade moved forward to reconnoiter the Confederate line, with skirmishers out front. They moved south along and to the west of Mount Tabor Church Road. After a sharp skirmish that lasted

Brigadier General Nathaniel C. McLean. *Courtesy of National Archives.*

the rest of the afternoon, the brigade succeeded in forcing the Confederate skirmishers back into their main line. William Price of the 6th East Tennessee was on the skirmish line close to the enemy works. One poor wounded Rebel stranded between the lines begged pitifully for help, but both sides were too afraid to venture forth to help him. He called out that he was a member of Company F of the 24th Alabama. When Price's regiment was relieved and withdrew at 10:00 p.m., they "left the poor wounded man alone with his Maker in the dark and dreary woods." It had been a sharp skirmish as far as such fighting went. Price listed the casualties for his regiment during this small firefight as seven killed and eight wounded, a rather large proportion of dead to wounded. The skirmishers of the Twenty-Third Corps took up positions as close to Hindman and Cleburne's lines as the terrain permitted.[96]

When McLean moved forward, Bond's brigade moved up and occupied their works. Upon returning, McLean's men fell back behind them and reformed in support of Bond, effectively switching places. At dusk, Colonel Bond personally supervised the posting of the 107th Illinois on the skirmish line in a field across Mount Tabor Church Road. Four companies faced to the south at right angles to the end of the brigade lines. Three companies formed on the left of the first four, bending back and facing east. The seven advancing companies spread out in a skirmish line and dug rifle pits for protection. The final three companies of the regiment formed a reserve along the Dallas–Acworth Road. Union cavalry was supposed to extend the line to the north and northeast along the same road.[97]

With the wagons and baggage trains of the Twentieth and his own Fourteenth Corps out of the way and moved up to Burnt Hickory, General Palmer was able to march his corps toward the front. They began moving at 1:00 a.m. and reached Burnt Hickory just before daylight. Continuing on, they stopped two miles south of the village for further instructions. Thomas ordered Johnson's First Division forward to support the Fourth Corps but left the Third Division behind at Burnt Hickory to guard the army's wagons. This resulted in the three divisions of the corps being widely separated, with the First Division at New Hope Church, the Third at Burnt Hickory and the Second near Dallas with McPherson. General Palmer tendered his resignation at the indignity of the dispersal of his corps. Thomas declined, but a conflict in orders and seniority in rank would bring a similar resignation from Palmer in August before Atlanta.[98]

Johnson's men continued forward, crossing Pumpkinvine Creek and marching in rear of the Fourth Corps toward the army's flank. General Thomas led the way in person. When they came upon the clear valley of Possum Creek, possibly in rear of Newton's division, the vanguard spotted a group of Confederate officers in a field some distance away. According to Henry Perry of the 38th Indiana,

> *General Thomas, who was near the head of our column, ordered the captain of one of our batteries to bring forward a gun. When this was*

done, the General hastily dismounted, sighted the gun, told the cannoneer how to cut his fuse for the distance, and gave the command to fire. The shell exploded in the midst of the Rebel horsemen, with what result is not known, except that there was an abrupt closing of the caucus and a rapid "skedaddling" of the Johnnies to some place beyond the reach of Yankee shells. This episode was very amusing on our side, because none of us had ever seen "Pap" Thomas do anything in a hurry.[99]

Apparently, firing individual cannon was a relaxing diversion from the stress of command for general officers. After this amusing episode, the division continued marching until it reached the vicinity of Brown's Mill, where it lay in reserve for the rest of the day.[100]

At Dallas, the Army of the Tennessee deployed in the morning and advanced on the town. Encountering only minor resistance, McPherson's men took control of the town and continued eastward. On the hills east of town, they ran up against Cheatham and Bate, strongly entrenched upon the heights. The Federals deployed north and south of the town to envelope the Confederate position, and late in the day, the Fourteenth Corps' Second Division under Brigadier General Jefferson C. Davis joined them. Davis's men extended the line east, but he didn't have enough men to fully connect with Hooker near New Hope Church three miles away.[101]

The fight during the morning and afternoon convinced Howard, Thomas and Sherman that they were opposite the right end of the Confederate line. And they were correct—at least for a short while. The movement of two Union corps did not go unnoticed, of course, and during the morning, Hood ordered General Hindman to shift his division from the left of Hood's Corps to its right. Hindman's arrival extended the Confederate line from the valley of Possum Creek to high ground along Mount Tabor Church Road, matching the Union extensions. The 24th Alabama that William Price had encountered during McLean's late afternoon advance was part of Hindman's command.[102]

Reinforcements were on the way. Johnston ordered Walker's Division to New Hope Church to reinforce Hood. Cleburne's men began their march at 4:00 a.m. as ordered by Hardee the previous evening and reached the Maulding house at 6:30 in the morning. There Walker received orders to move to the right of Hindman and lengthen the line even further. Once they reached the front at New Hope Church, they turned right and moved to the northeast. Captain Foster notes that while they were moving behind the lines, they were still in danger with "an occasional bullet whistling past, like it was on the hunt of some one." While on the march, some of Foster's regiment ventured up to the frontline to see what soldiers were there "because they have no confidence in any of them except Arkansas troops. We find Georgia troops to our front; and our boys tell them that if they run that we will shoot them, and no mistake, and as soon as they find out that the Texans are in their rear, they believe we will shoot them sure enough."[103]

Private Smith and his wagon had an equally harrowing encounter, as they passed in range of a Union battery while on the move. The division reached its position at the end of the line at two or three o'clock in the afternoon, and Smith's wagon train parked and made camp about three hundred yards behind the division lines. Cleburne posted Polk's Brigade on the frontline immediately to the right of Hindman's Division, on the east side of Mount Tabor Church Road. The brigade was deployed along a ridge, and its right ended at a large wheat field. Immediately behind the brigade was a winding road leading generally east along the ridge. About a mile east of its intersection with Mount Tabor Church Road the road crossed a creek near the farm and mill owned by the widow of Benjamin Pickett, a Confederate soldier killed at Chickamauga. The road was therefore appropriately named Pickett's Mill Road, as the creek was just as aptly named Pickett's Mill Creek. Cleburne stationed Hotchkiss's artillery battalion to the right of Polk and one regiment of Govan's Brigade next to Hotchkiss to guard the extreme end of the line. The rest of the division formed a second line behind Polk and Hindman, from left to right, Lowrey, Granbury and Govan. Brigadier General John H. Kelly's cavalry division held the ridge between Cleburne's right and Pickett's Mill Creek. At least one regiment from Granbury's Brigade was detached and moved over to the right to help bolster the cavalry.[104]

Polk and Hotchkiss immediately began digging in along the northern crest of the ridge. Smith spent the afternoon issuing ammunition from his wagon to the men in the frontline trenches. During the afternoon, he saw four Union prisoners on their way to the rear. He described them as "very young and tidy looking men, they have been in the service three years and have reenlisted for the war." He also noted the devastation the army had wrought on the surrounding landscape. This area of Georgia had previously been untouched by the war, yet after only two days of the Army of Tennessee being there it was "perfectly desolated for miles around by the army. Young crops ruined and turned out, fences burned, and general destruction."[105]

The day ended with the lines between the two combatants roughly completed. Johnston had men entrenched from Dallas to just west of Pickett's Mill Creek, with a gap between Bate's Division of Hardee's Corps and Polk's Corps near New Hope Church. Likewise, the Union armies stretched from Dallas to the Mount Tabor Church Road, with a similar gap between Davis's division and Hooker at New Hope Church. Neither side was aware of the gap in the other's line. Sherman, at least, was none too concerned. He planned on shifting his lines the next day and reuniting the armies. Unfortunately, this would prove to be much more difficult than any of the Union commanders imagined.

Chapter 8

Those Damned Bugles

Friday, May 27 "dawned clear and gave promise of a bright warm day." Reveille sounded at 3:30 a.m. for the 79th Indiana, and the cooks issued two days worth of beef rations. The rest of Wood's division probably awoke at the same time, the men prepared for the tasks ahead of them.[106]

Sherman had outlined the responsibilities for each command the night before. Late in the evening, he had issued Special Field Order No. 12. First, the artillery of Hooker, Howard and Schofield's command would open a bombardment early in the morning, continuing until 9:00 a.m. Then at 10:00 a.m., Howard's Fourth Corps was to advance down the east side of Possum Creek and take the high ground at the intersection of Mount Tabor Church Road and Pickett's Mill Road, since they thought the Confederate line terminated near there. The Twenty-Third Corps would support Howard's movement, and Hooker would try to take some portion of the Rebel works to his front as a diversion. Finally, Davis and McPherson were to attack straight toward New Hope Church, through the Confederates confronting them if necessary, and link up with Hooker.[107]

As ordered, the three corps in front of New Hope Church began their bombardment of the Confederate lines as early as 5:20 a.m. Battery after battery pounded the enemy lines. The Rebels responded in kind, and soon the air was full of exploding shells. When a battery in Wood's sector failed to commence firing on time, he sent Major James B. Hampson, an aide-de-camp on detached duty from the 124th Ohio, to hurry them up. While helping them get ready, a sharpshooter's bullet struck him in the left shoulder and broke his spine. He was then carried to the rear, where he clung to life until 4:00 p.m. that afternoon. A very popular young officer, many of the division mentioned his death in their official reports and regimental histories. Howard, who thought Wood was always in control of himself, was surprised when he saw that officer sitting next to his dying aide and weeping openly. Captain Lewis of the 124th Ohio described him as "one of the most intelligent, soldierly and brave officers in the 4th Army Corps. He was, without doubt, the best drilled man in the Third Division."[108]

At about 7:00 a.m., Howard ordered Wood's division to pack up and march to the rear. Howard had selected them to spearhead the day's assault. Wood objected, stating that his men had fought hard for the position and had spent all night working on their trenches and that it was their turn to rest. Howard told Wood and Hazen, who was also present, that he had selected the division because in his belief it "gave the greatest promise of succeeding in the work in hand." Flattery or not, Wood acquiesced, and the remark forestalled any objection on the part of the normally temperamental Hazen. As Wood's men filed out of their trenches, Stanley's division moved up from behind Newton and took their place, perhaps enjoying the fact that there were no more comfortable works than those built by somebody else. They left the artillery in position. Meanwhile, Thomas and Howard rode forward to have a look at the ground on which they were supposed to attack.[109]

The Federals weren't the only ones making preparations for the day. Since his works did not confront the enemy directly, General Cleburne ordered Govan at 7:00 a.m. to take his brigade north outside the lines, swing west and reconnoiter the enemy. Govan's men dutifully moved from their position behind Polk and Hotchkiss, crossed over the breastworks and moved into empty space between the lines. After swinging west and crashing through the thick underbrush, they eventually came upon a field near the Dallas–Acworth Road.[110]

Captain Thomas J. Milholand of the 107th Illinois heard them coming. He commanded the three left companies of the regiment facing east. Cautioning his men, he advanced alone a few rods (a rod is equal to 5.5 yards) for a better look. As he listened, Confederate skirmishers emerged from the underbrush in front of him. They saw Milholand and opened fire. The captain's fortune was good, and he escaped, while the Union skirmishers in their rifle pits immediately returned fire. The entire Rebel skirmish line responded with a volley. The Confederate fire revealed that the three left companies of the 107th were in trouble—the Rebel line extended past their flank. The commander of the 107th, Major Uriah M. Laurance, took immediate action. He ordered the two leftmost companies to abandon

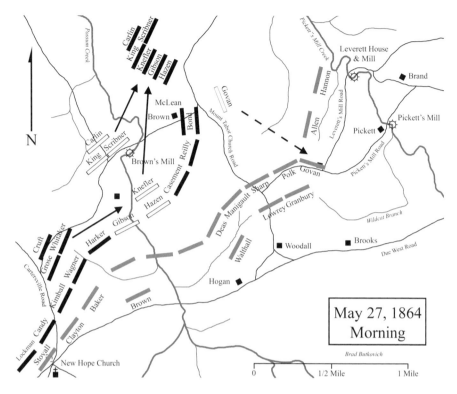

Moving into position on the morning of May 27. *Courtesy of the author.*

their rifle pits and pull back about 60 yards to another low ridge. He then deployed his reserves. One company went to the extreme left to match the line of the Confederates, while another went to the center with orders to reinforce the line or if not needed there to report to the extreme left. The final company of the reserves moved to the intersection of Mount Tabor Church Road, about the center of the regiment's line, and began building a line of barricades.[111]

Part of Govan's line extended over the Dallas–Acworth Road and approached the Union lines from the north. The cavalry Major Laurance thought was supposed to be guarding that area was nowhere to be seen. The Confederates pressed the left companies hard. Like a giant game of cat-and-mouse, the two sides fired at each other from behind trees, rocks or any cover they could find. To relieve the pressure, Laurance ordered a counterattack, hoping to recapture the rifle pits they had abandoned that morning. The men dashed forward and secured their previous position, but the Rebels reformed and quickly advanced again. As they had in the morning, the Confederate line was longer than the Union's, and Major Laurance ordered the men to once again leave their rifle pits and fall back to the second line.[112]

While Govan was working over the 107th, Thomas and Howard were riding south toward the heights along Mount Tabor Church Road. While riding between the lines somewhere near the road, Thomas and Howard came to a large open field. There they made a startling discovery. The Confederate lines extended much farther to the east than they had the day before—thanks to Hindman and Cleburne's redeployments. If Howard and Cox attacked due south along the road, they would be making a frontal assault against prepared earthworks. Not wanting a repeat of the bloody assault two days ago, Thomas changed the plan of attack. He ordered Howard "to move General Wood farther to the left and beyond all troops and endeavor to strike the enemy's flank." To strengthen the attack, Thomas placed Johnson's Fourteenth Corps division, located nearby at Brown's Mill, under Howard's command. The two divisions probably numbered about 12,500 men in the ranks after three weeks of campaigning.[113]

Meanwhile, the 107th Illinois was struggling to hold its position at the extreme left of the army. More enemy troops were moving to the left. Major Laurance reported at least one of Govan's regiments formed in line of battle supporting the skirmishers. Colonel Bond mentioned seeing three regiments, but it was not clear if he meant in line of battle or altogether throughout the entire morning. With the new enemy line once again threatened to overlap his left, Laurance had his left companies withdraw to yet another new position. He thought it a good one and hoped to counterattack and regain the morning's first line if he could get reinforcements.[114] Those reinforcements arrived at 10:00 a.m. in the form of the 23rd Michigan, which Colonel Bond sent forward to bolster the beleaguered 107th. The 23rd lined up on the left of the 107th, with four companies in front as skirmishers. The remaining four companies formed behind them in column by division, meaning that each company formed a column four men wide and lined up side by side. This narrow formation allowed the reserve companies to march quickly and deploy into other formations, such as a line of battle, very quickly. As soon as the 23rd was on line with the left of the 107th, Major Laurance ordered an attack to regain the morning's line. The two regiments advanced and swung to the right, but the 23rd took fire from the left flank and fell back. This exposed the flank of the 107th, so they too had to abandon the attack. The two regiments settled back down where they had started, the 107th's third line, and traded shots with the Rebels for an hour.[115]

Present-day image of the ford at Brown's Mill looking east. *Author's collection*.

Colonel Bond wasn't ready to surrender the field to the Confederates. About 11:00 p.m., he sent the 111th Ohio into the fray. They moved up to relieve the four right companies of the 107th, who were still in their original position and hadn't come under attack all morning. The 111th relieved the 107th, but not before losing one man killed and ten wounded due to a faulty deployment. The four unengaged companies of the 107th quickly moved to the left. Major Laurance put two of them on the main line to bolster its strength and had the other two build a second line to the rear.[116]

The Confederate accounts of this skirmish are much less detailed. One of Govan's men wrote in his dairy that they drove back two lines of skirmishers one mile. Another mentions the back-and-forth nature of the fight, with the Rebels sometimes retiring and other times pushing back the Federals in turn. Eventually, they pushed the enemy back into their main works, which could certainly have occurred at some part of the line. However, by that time, the main threat to the Union position was over. Govan's skirmishers had throughout the morning noticed Federal soldiers moving past their right, a fact of which he dutifully notified Cleburne. At 9:50 a.m., Hood sent Cleburne a message indicating that he could withdraw Govan if the move did not attract special attention from the Federals. So, at about the same time the 111th Ohio was entering the battle, Cleburne sent an order to Govan to leave his skirmishers out front and have the rest of his brigade rejoin the division. His mission had been accomplished.[117]

In fact, Govan had already decided to return on his own. Confusing reports from the cavalry to his right left him with the impression that his flank was unguarded. Without orders, he withdrew his brigade to the northern edge of the large wheat field to the right of Polk. The general left his brigade to report to Cleburne and on the way encountered an officer from Cleburne's staff. The staff officer directed Govan to return his skirmishers to the site of the morning's skirmish, which he did. Once he reached Cleburne's headquarters, Govan explained the reasons for his withdrawal. Cleburne, of course, had ordered the withdrawal at the same time, so he did nothing to censure his brigadier. However, he did permit Govan to move his brigade back to the southern end of the wheat field, link up with Polk's Brigade to the left and begin digging in.[118]

The men Govan's skirmishers had seen moving past them were the divisions of Wood and Johnson. Howard needed a place where he could form up his two divisions for the attack, and he selected a large field on the extreme left and rear of the Twenty-Third Corps. The exact location of this field has been lost to time, but it must have been northeast of the intersection of the Mount Tabor Church and Dallas–Acworth Roads, perhaps by as much as half a mile. The men arrived at about 10:00 a.m. and quickly formed for the advance. General Wood formed his division in a column of brigades. Each brigade formed its regiments into two lines, half in the frontline and half in the second. The brigades then lined up one behind the other. The end result was a narrow column of infantry six lines deep. Theoretically, such a narrow column of infantry enabled better command and control while on the march, and in the attack, such a deep mass of men should be able to overwhelm the enemy at any given point. However, that same narrowness also made it susceptible to fire from the flanks. In fact, Hooker had used this very formation at New Hope Church two days before and had suffered heavy casualties.[119]

Each brigade commander used his own discretion in leading and organizing the regiments in his brigade. Giving orders to seven or more maneuver elements in a command is no easy task, and each commander in Wood's division handled it differently. General Hazen and his Second Brigade were in the lead. There were eight regiments in his brigade, and he deployed four in the front rank and four in the rear. In addition, he coupled two regiments together under one commanding officer and called them battalions. That way, he only had to issue orders to four officers instead of eight. In the brigade frontline, from left to right, the 124th Ohio formed a battalion with the 93rd Ohio. Next to it, the 41st and 1st Ohio regiments formed another. The second line consisted of the 6th and 23rd Kentucky on the left and the 6th Indiana and 5th Kentucky on the right. As the first brigade of the division, skirmishers from several of Hazen's regiments would lead the advance. The frontline regiments each contributed individual companies to the brigade skirmish line, among them was Captain Lewis of the 124th Ohio and his Company B. Major John H. Williston of the 41st Ohio took command of the frontline skirmishers.[120] The next brigade in the column was Colonel Gibson's First Brigade. The frontline had the 32nd Indiana on the left, the 15th Wisconsin in the center and the 89th Illinois on the right. The second line consisted of the 49th Ohio on the left, the 35th Illinois in the middle and the 15th Ohio on the right. With only six regiments, Colonel Gibson elected to exercise direct command over each unit.[121]

The last brigade in Wood's division was Colonel Knefler's Third Brigade, which he split into demi-brigades. The first line of regiments formed one demi-brigade and the second line the other. The first line had the 86th Indiana on the right, followed by the 59th Ohio, 13th Ohio and, finally, the 17th Kentucky on the left. Colonel Alexander M. Stout of the 17th Kentucky commanded this demi-brigade. The rear demi-brigade, commanded by Colonel Charles F. Manderson of the 19th Ohio, had the 19th Ohio on the right, the 79th Indiana in the center and the 9th Kentucky on the left. Each of the two rear brigades of the division had skirmishers out on the flanks to prevent surprises from either direction.[122] Johnson's division formed behind Wood. General King's Second Brigade, the Regulars, took up a position immediately behind Knefler. Colonel Scribner's Third Brigade deployed to the left of King, and General Carlin's First Brigade followed the first two in support.[123]

By 11:00 a.m., the divisions had formed and were ready to advance. Hazen and his regimental commanders were called together to meet with Howard, Wood and Johnson. Wood personally gave a pocket compass to Lieutenant Colonel Robert L. Kimberly of the 41st Ohio, in command of the battalion consisting of the 1st and 41st Ohio, presumably to give or help Major Williston lead the brigade. Kimberly later wrote that Wood told him to move due southeast and then turn and move southwest until the enemy was found. Wood expressed the hope that they would find the Confederate rear or, failing that, fall on the Rebel flank. Wood was emphatic on one point: they were to "attack the instant the enemy was found, waiting for no further orders under any circumstances, whether the enemy were found in position or not, behind fortifications or otherwise." Wood's parting words were an admonition that five other brigades were behind him, a not so subtle hint to avoid botching his assignment.[124]

The large open field where the command assembled, beyond and behind the rest of the army, was still a dangerous place. Govan's skirmishers were not far away. While the men of Scribner's brigade waited, a squad from the 2nd Ohio brought in the body of Captain R.J. Waggener, assistant adjutant general of Carlin's brigade. A single bullet fired by a nearby Rebel had killed him. It was turning out to be a bad day for staff officers, and it would only get worse.[125]

To the south, Cleburne continued his preparations. His eye for terrain and how it influenced the flow of battle served him well. Hotchkiss's artillery was stationed at the southwest corner of a large wheat field, bordered by a fence, and Pickett's Mill Road ran behind them. When Govan's Brigade returned, Cleburne posted them at the southern end of this field, where they built breastworks. At the southeast corner was a "T" intersection in the road, and another road ran north along the eastern boundary of the field, on top of a spur ridge running north to south. This road eventually crossed Pickett's Mill Creek at a house and mill owned by J.C. Leverette. Pickett's Mill Road continued east from the intersection along the ridge, but immediately northeast of the intersection was the head of a large ravine. For about the first two hundred yards, the ravine was a relatively shallow bowl, but afterward, it turned right and plunged into a deep gorge. A small stream at its base eventually emptied into Pickett's Mill Creek. The underbrush was thick inside the ravine but thinned as it neared the crest. Rock outcroppings large and small dotted the slopes. Cleburne saw that an enemy force trying to move past his right flank would have to cross the ravine. Govan's rightmost regiment, the 6th & 7th Arkansas, was bent back from the main line. Its left wing could fire down into the ravine and hit any unit trying to cross it in the flank and rear. Its right wing ended at the head of the ravine, and with it the division's line. Cleburne ordered Hotchkiss to station artillery at the head of the ravine too, and the artillery commander dispatched a section of two twelve-pounder howitzers from Key's battery to that location. The artillerists made a breach in the earthworks in the middle of the 6th & 7th and placed the section of howitzers to fire down the length of the ravine. Any Union troops crossing the ravine would receive a devastating barrage of shot, shell and canister in the flank. Cleburne also foresaw the need to move troops rapidly to the right if it became necessary to extend his line and ordered

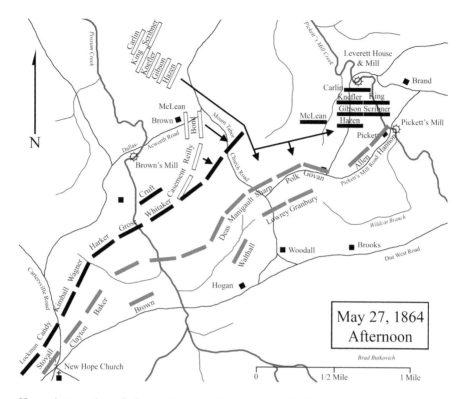

Howard moves through the woods toward the end of the Confederate lines on the afternoon of May 27. *Courtesy of the author.*

details to cut connecting trails behind each brigade. He also had trails cut off to the right behind Kelly's cavalry. He didn't ignore logistics either. Several of his men were armed with the highly accurate Whitworth rifle, and he tried to get one of his aides, Major Calhoun Benham, to secure more of its unique ammunition.[126]

While these preparations were going on at the division level, some of Granbury's men found free time to explore. Lieutenant R.M. Collins of the 6th & 15th Texas and a few of his men went to the right of the brigade line and snooped around the farmhouse at the intersection of Pickett's Mill and Leverett's Mill Roads near Key's howitzers. The Picketts owned the property but rented out this farm to another family. But with Cleburne's men digging breastworks just yards from the house, the family undoubtedly found it a dangerous place to be. Upon searching the house and grounds, Collins and his men found that the owners had tried to hide their valuables before leaving. They found a feather bed and several other household goods stashed in the nearby well.[127]

Captain Foster was also busy that morning. General Granbury called for a scouting party of five men to go around the Yankee army, and presumably Govan's men too. Colonel Wilkes of the 24th & 25th Texas ordered Foster to detail men from his company for the assignment. They headed out early and wouldn't be back until later that afternoon.[128]

Teamster Smith spent the morning at General Johnson's headquarters at the William Wigley house near New Hope Church. Even though they were three quarters of a mile behind the lines, they were still not completely safe. A Union battery was "firing furiously" in their direction, and Smith saw two horses badly wounded by a shell. As a precaution, the wagon train was moved. While near army headquarters, Smith heard that the 48th Tennessee was nearby. In an odd administrative quirk, there were actually two 48th Tennessee regiments in Confederate service. They started out as the same unit, but early in the war, half of the regiment was captured at Fort Donelson in February 1862. There were enough men on sick leave and detached service outside the fort, plus some extra companies added from other regiments, to continue the existence of the 48th. It became known as the 48th Tennessee (Nixon), after its new commander, Colonel George H. Nixon. It eventually became part of Cleburne's Division, and Smith belonged to this unit. The new arrival was the 48th Tennessee (Voorhies), which was composed primarily of those captured at Fort Donelson, exchanged and returned to service. Smith wanted to visit the new arrivals, but since times were critical, he didn't take the chance.[129]

The 48th Tennessee (Voorhies) had just arrived that morning as part of a brigade commanded by Brigadier General William A. Quarles. The brigade, a mix of Louisiana and Tennessee regiments that had been captured and exchanged at least once during the war, had collectively seen battle in only minor actions at Baton Rouge, Jackson, a few at Fort Donelson and one at Shiloh. None had seen anything more than a skirmish in ten months. They had transferred from Mobile as reinforcements for the Army of Tennessee and had only unloaded from the trains in Marietta the night before. After an eighteen-mile all-night march, they arrived at the army on the morning of the twenty-seventh. The brigade consisted of the 4th and 30th Louisiana regiments, as well as the 42nd, 46th & 55th, 48th (Voorhies), 49th and 53rd Tennessee regiments.[130]

To the north, about 11:00 a.m., Howard ordered the ad-hoc corps forward. Accounts of the direction (or directions) in which the column marched are as varied as the recollections of how far they marched. General Wood and the regimental history of the 79th Indiana agree that they went one mile south before turning and going a mile and a half west for a total of two and a half miles. However, Wood then writes that they continued east to get to the end of the Confederate line. It is also possible that the committee that wrote the 79th history used Wood's report for the information. In his report, Colonel Oliver H. Payne of the 124th Ohio wrote that they traveled a total of two miles, while Colonel Gibson remembered two and a half miles. For a differing view, Colonel Scribner said they first traveled east until they met the enemy's trenches, then north, then east again. Howard also thought that they first marched east. On the extreme, Sergeant Gregory C. McDermott of the 23rd Kentucky thought they traveled four miles. It's possible that the longer accounts of distance included the march to the assembly area beyond the Twenty-Third Corps.[131]

Careful examination of a map will show that the column did most likely march in a southeastern direction about a mile, skirting the right of Hascall's Twenty-Third Corps division and the end of the Union line. It probably traveled along the axis of the Dallas–Acworth Road/Mount Tabor Church Road for at least part of the march. It then ran up against the breastworks manned by Hindman and Polk, backed up, turned left, and continued toward the end of the Rebel line. It may have even stopped and turned left more than once. Altogether, it can be extremely difficult to gauge distances while traveling through dense underbrush and up and down ravines and spurs with frequent stops and starts all the while sweating in the hot sun under several pounds of equipment.

As soon as the march began, the skirmishers of the 41st Ohio out in front passed pickets of the Twenty-Third Corps at the edge of the field they had assembled in, possibly from the left of the line held by the 23rd Michigan. The Ohio men plunged into the woods and soon encountered Rebel skirmishers on their right flank. The Confederates killed one man and wounded another in Captain James McMahon's Company A in this initial clash. The captain ordered the company to wheel to the right and push forward. They did so, and the Confederate pickets fell back before them. They continued pursuing the Rebels until they came to a field with the enemy works on the other side. Twenty-Third Corps skirmishers came up behind them in relief, and McMahon led his company to the left to rejoin the column.[132]

The rest of the two divisions struggled behind them. As the column passed by Bond's three regiments out in front, the skirmishers Govan left behind retired, and Major Laurance was able to advance his 107th Illinois and retake his first line from earlier in the morning. Shortly afterward, the three regiments received orders to fall back into the brigade's main earthworks.[133]

With everyone deployed in line of battle, marching through the wilderness was no easy task for Howard's column. Frequent halts were ordered to address the lines and keep everybody in formation. Many in the rank and file thought that the march to find the Rebel flank was supposed to catch the enemy by surprise. But to their consternation, the buglers of Gibson's brigade continued to blow and give orders. Sergeant Arnold Brandley of the 23rd Kentucky noted, "The command were imparted by the Headquarters bugler of Willich's or Beatty's Brigade. That organization drilled chiefly by bugle calls; consequently each regimental and company bugler repeated the orders from Headquarters, making it a perfect din of sounds." Sergeant McDermott, also in the 23rd, was a little more disagreeable. "We objected to it on account of it attracting the Johnnies shells so often," he wrote, "for every now and then, one would burst over head, breaking the branches of the trees and causing a scattering." Alexis Cope, in Gibson's own brigade, probably summed it up best when he lamented, "More than one officer and man exclaimed: 'If we are expected to surprise the enemy, why don't they stop those d—d bugles?' But on we went, our bugles blowing. Even when we halted for a short rest, the bugles sounded the long drawn out note which commanded us to stop." The Union men didn't know it, but thanks to their skirmishers and scouts, the Confederates knew where they were with or without the bugle calls.[134]

It may have taken as much as two hours to march the first mile, but about that time, the skirmishers of the 41st Ohio ran headlong into a line of rifle pits. Unfortunately, they were facing the wrong direction. The column had run into the Twenty-Third Corps' skirmishers at the end of the Union line. The rest of the Twenty-Third Corps had also been on the move. As Howard's men passed them, or shortly thereafter, General Cox gave the order to advance the corps, which then pivoted on its right flank, moved to face due south instead of east and marched as close to the enemy's works as the terrain permitted. There the corps began the process of digging in a new line.[135]

Despite Wood's admonition to Colonel Kimberly to "attack the instant the enemy was found," the men did not charge past the end of the line to assault the Confederate position head on. Instead, Howard had the men retire a short distance to the rear, face to the left and continue east toward what he hoped was the end of the Rebel line. As he was in the process of re-orienting his troops, General McLean, of the Twenty-Third Corps, was ordered to use his brigade to maintain contact with Howard. Exactly who gave the order is unclear. In his report, Howard merely mentioned that McLean deployed so as to form a junction but does not say that he issued the order and took command of a brigade from another corps. General Cox states in his report that McLean's brigade was ordered to support a movement made by Howard. The Fourth Corps journal kept at headquarters agrees, though it doesn't mention McLean by name. This leads to the conclusion that the order perhaps came from someone higher up, probably Thomas. If that was the case, it was the only time during the march and later battle that Thomas had a hand in coordinating the movement. Otherwise, Howard was on his own.[136]

Off to the left they marched. Two divisions stopped at least one more time, turned south and marched until they encountered enemy works, possibly several times. During one of these stops to test the Confederate lines, impatience wrecked the column's formation. Johnson, irritated with the frequent stops and starts, pulled Scribner aside. In a polite voice that Scribner recognized as laced with frustration, the division commander asked, "Will you be so kind as to move south until I tell you to halt?" Scribner answered in the affirmative, and with the help of an aid and his compass, the brigade marched south. Unfortunately, being at the rear of the column meant that the brigade had to march through the men in front of them. This Scribner's men did, much to the consternation of the rest of the column. After reaching the front, Scribner reined in his horse next to Howard, who was busy studying the Confederate line in the distance, and explained his orders. Howard told him that it would be "unsafe to advance further" and that they would resume the march to the left. At that time, Johnson rode up, and he and Howard discussed the matter further. Scribner returned to his brigade, which resumed its station in the column, probably by waiting until Wood's men had passed and then falling back into its proper place.[137]

Lieutenant Woodcock of the 9th Kentucky described marching "over rough hills, across deep hollows, and through almost impenetrable thickets of undergrowth for about three or four miles without meeting with any opposition, and I was almost coming to the conclusion that we were destined to surprise the enemy at some point where they did not expect us." Members of the 79th Indiana remembered going "through dense forests and the thickest jungles, over a country scarred by deep ravines and intersected by difficult ridges. Added to these difficulties, the hot rays of a tropical sun made it almost impossible to advance under such adverse circumstances."[138]

During the move east, the column came upon a small field, and Howard, Johnson and Wood stopped to observe the enemy on the opposite side.

Howard's aide, Captain Harry M. Stinson, wanted to try out his new field glass. Howard had warned him and other members of his staff not to needlessly expose themselves, but Stinson boldly stepped out into the open. No sooner had he raised the glass to his forehead than the dull thud of a bullet striking flesh gave credence to Howard's warning. In fact, Johnson recalled hearing two thuds—one when Stinson was hit and another when the round hit an oak tree behind them. When Howard looked over, he saw that Stinson had fallen forward onto his face. He had been shot through the lungs and had a bullet hole in his back, the round having passed clean through his body. Howard and Wood carried Stinson to the rear and called for a stretcher. It looked as though he would go into shock, and Howard knelt beside him, speaking words of encouragement. Wood obtained a canteen of whiskey from a staff officer and gave about a half pint to the wounded man. It revived him enough to ask for another half pint as the stretcher-bearers were carrying him off. Wood obliged, and Stinson departed. He survived and remarkably returned to service on Howard's staff just two months later.[139]

Eventually, a little before 4:00 p.m., the lead elements of the column made their way down a long slope, crossed a small tributary of Pickett's Mill Creek and ascended the opposite hill. The column came to a halt on a small hilltop at the summit. The Leverett's Mill Road ran past their right toward the south. Pickett's Mill Creek was at the bottom of the hill to the left. The surrounding woods were open, with little underbrush, and the southern slope of the hill terminated at a large wheat field. Howard, Johnson and Wood went forward to the edge of the field to investigate. They found there "a line of works to our right, but they did not seem to cover General Wood's front, and they were new, the enemy still working hard upon them." What they observed was Govan's men busily constructing their works.[140]

Howard had finally found the end of the Confederate line.

Chapter 9

Criminal Blunder

After observing the fresh earthworks and the Confederates working on them, Howard sent off a note to Thomas at 3:35 p.m.:

> *GENERAL: I am on the ridge beyond the field that we were looking at this morning. No person can appreciate the difficulty in moving over this ground unless he can see it. I am on the east side of the creek on which Pettit's [Pickett's] Mill is, facing south, and am now turning the enemy's right flank, I think. A prisoner reports two divisions in front of us, Cleburne's and Hindman's.*
>
> *Very respectfully,*
> *O.O. HOWARD,*
> *Major-General.*
> *Cox must move up to the open field to connect with us as soon as possible.*

From this note, it's clear that Howard was still unsure if they had reached the Confederate flank. Whether such a hesitant declaration filled Thomas with confidence in his subordinate remains unknown. Still, the time had come to stop marching and start fighting. Thomas sent the staff officer back to Howard with a note that read, "Major-General Sherman wishes us to get on the enemy's right flank and rear as soon as possible." That is, get on with the attack.[141]

Howard ordered the column to wheel to the right and face southward. It was no easy task reorienting twelve thousand men in the woods and up and down the slopes of the ridgeline. It took time. Also, not all of the regiments made it to the assembly area at full strength. The 13th and 59th Ohio, both in Knefler's brigade, formed up with only eight companies on line. Each regiment had contributed two companies to the skirmish line on the march, and they had been left behind. They would not rejoin their units until after nightfall. Eventually, the men got into position. Hazen's Second Brigade was still in the front, followed by Gibson's First Brigade and Knefler's Third. Johnson's division moved to the left, between Wood and Pickett's Mill Creek. Johnson ordered Scribner's Third Brigade to move up alongside Gibson's to protect Wood's flank when the latter advanced. There wasn't enough room between Wood and the creek to deploy his whole brigade, so Scribner formed up perpendicular to Wood, facing east. The creek veered upstream to the left, so when Wood advanced, Scribner planned to shake his brigade out into line as more room became available. On the southern slope of the hill in front of Scribner stood a small wheat field, and at the bottom of the hill was the creek that flowed through the ravine. The field continued past the other side of the stream and up the opposite slope before ending at another wood line. A fence bordered the entire field. Near where the creek flowed into Pickett's Mill Creek stood the Pickett house and mill. Kelly's cavalry occupied the ridge to the front. Across the creek from Scribner was a broad draw, and to the south of the draw, the ridge that Kelly's men were deployed on continued on the east side. Johnson ordered King's Second Brigade behind Scribner to support him, while Carlin's First Brigade remained in the rear on the north slope of the hill. After Wood was in place, Howard allowed them time to rest, though Johnson's men were still on the move attempting to get into position. The skirmishers of the 41st and 124th Ohio were still out front, and the occasional crack of a skirmisher's rifle broke the tranquility and reminded them the enemy was nearby.[142]

Cleburne knew they were there. You can't hide the presence of a corps of infantry only seven hundred yards away. Captain Foster's scouting party had returned with reports of the progress of their march. So too had Govan's skirmishers and Kelly's cavalrymen, who kept a close eye on the moving column. During the morning, most of the two small brigades of Kelly's Division under Colonel Moses Hannon and Brigadier General William Allen had been busy digging rifle pits from the end of Cleburne's line to the creek. At the beginning of the campaign, these two brigades could only muster roughly 1,405 men present for duty, of which only 994 were available for the firing line.

Given that the campaign was three weeks old and some casualties, desertions and detachments would have depleted the regiments, they could have had fewer. General Wheeler, who was coordinating the Confederate cavalry on the far right flank of the entire army, put the number at 822. On the other hand, Wheeler had understated his strength before in order to magnify his own accomplishments, so it's entirely possible that he had more men than reported. He could have merely included in that number those actively engaged at any one time. With poor recordkeeping, it's almost impossible to get an accurate number of the cavalry engaged in the battle. Regardless of the actual number, Kelly had far too few men to resist Howard's men. Seeing the pressure Kelly was facing, Wheeler ordered a brigade from Brigadier General William Y.C. Hume's cavalry division to deploy on the ridge on the east side of the creek across from the mill.[143] In fact, some of them were still behind Howard. Some of Knefler's men, at the rear of the column, spotted Confederate scouts behind them. Without orders, many of them faced to the rear and fired a scattered volley in their direction, causing the Rebels to "scamper off in splendid style." The Yanks laughed as they fled.[144]

While Howard had been moving east, McLean and his men were struggling to follow their orders to provide a link between Howard and Bond's brigades at the end of the main Union line. At the very least, the gap between the two forces was half a mile, and maybe closer to three quarters. McLean marched most of the brigade alongside Howard and detached skirmishers to keep connected with Bond. When Howard stopped and assembled his command facing south, McLean formed his command facing south behind and to the right of Wood.[145]

Howard now had to decide on his next course of action. Sherman's orders had tasked the Fourth and Twenty-Third Corps to advance down Mount Tabor Church Road and seize the high ground to the south. Howard and Thomas's early morning reconnaissance revealed the impracticality of this and necessitated a change in plan. Thomas then ordered Howard to take a division from his corps and another from the Fourteenth Corps and march past the end of the Union line, find the end of the Confederates' and attack the enemy's flank.

Howard dutifully complied, but his first attempt at navigating through the backwoods of Paulding County was a failure, taking him longer than expected. His men were understandably tired if not exhausted. After reforming and getting into position, it was nearly four o'clock in the afternoon. There were only three hours left before sunset and another thirty minutes of twilight afterward before total darkness came at eight o'clock. It would become hard

Pre-war photo of Brigadier General Thomas J. Wood. *Courtesy of Library of Congress.*

to see much earlier than that with the smoke from thousands of muskets. He would have to attack, break through the enemy's defenses, consolidate his gains and reform his attacking force against a possible enemy counterattack before nightfall—all the while isolated from the main body of his army. That's a pretty daunting prospect for any general.

Howard had three options. He could aggressively launch most of his command at the enemy, perhaps prudently leaving a brigade behind as a last reserve. In fact, his commanding officer had just sent him a message telling him to make an attack of some kind. This option obviously had the most to gain, but it also had the most to lose. If he drove the Confederates away from their position, he could place himself beyond the end of the Confederate line. Once there, he would threaten the Due West Road, only half a mile away, with no defensible terrain feature in between. This would cut off the direct route to Acworth and Allatoona and leave Johnston only the Dallas road as an open route to Marietta. However, if the attack failed, Howard would find himself isolated from the rest of the Union army with two divisions of tired, demoralized and disorganized men. A commanding officer had to expect an aggressive foe to counterattack and destroy or capture such a force. It takes a bold and aggressive general to take that kind of gamble. Unfortunately, nowhere in Howard's career had he exhibited that type of aggressiveness and daring.

His second option was to do nothing. He had prolonged the Union line considerably, and if reinforced, he could fill the gap between himself and the Twenty-Third Corps the next day. While prudent, it was not what Sherman or Thomas had ordered. Sherman had already taken Thomas to task for not attacking immediately at New Hope Church two days before. While this proved to be unfounded and unfair to Thomas at the time, Howard could only have taken it as a reprimand against an officer that Sherman deemed too slow or unwilling to bring on a battle. Since Sherman had sent him to find and attack the Confederate flank, to dig in without attacking would appear to Howard as a damaging or unwise career choice.

The third option was to attempt some course of action between the two. A reconnaissance-in-force would involve sending only a few of his units forward to feel out the Confederate defenses. If they were successful, then Howard could order more brigades into action to support a breakthrough. If not, he could call off his attack with minimal casualties (overall at least) and report the enemy too strong to assault. It would reconcile his desire for caution and Thomas's admonition to attack. This is the course of action Howard decided to take.

While Howard was making his decision, Wood's men waited in the hot sun. Lieutenant Ambrose Bierce, Hazen's topographical engineer and famous postwar author, crept forward to study the enemy position. He went far enough forward that he could hear the murmur of the Confederates ahead before returning to his own lines. Some soldiers cooked dinner—after all, they had marched all afternoon and hadn't had anything to eat since breakfast. Some found time to crack a joke or two. The birds were singing in the trees, and one soldier said it would be a pity to frighten them but by necessity there would be more or less noise soon. His comrades laughed. Others found time for a nap. W.S. Franklin of the 49th Ohio noted that when they later awoke, many claimed they had a premonition of a calamity ahead.[146] Some, like Sergeant Brandley, went in search of water to refill their canteens. Brandley strode down the hill to the small creek they had crossed earlier. As he was filling up, a group of officers gathered nearby and dismounted. Among those he recognized were Howard and Hazen, his brigade commander. Also in attendance were Wood and probably a few officers from their respective staffs, including Lieutenant Bierce. Wood remarked to Howard, "We will put in Hazen and see what success he has." Hazen was startled, to say the least. This seemed to imply that instead of a grand charge by an entire division in column supported by a second, Hazen's lead brigade would attack alone. His success would dictate the course of action afterward. Although the officers couldn't have known it at the time, instead of fourteen thousand in seven brigades against Cleburne's and Kelly's seven thousand, it would be Hazen's two thousand against seven thousand—quite a reversal. Brandley clearly heard Howard's next remark. "General," he said to Hazen, "you will have to charge and turn the enemy's flank if you sacrifice your brigade." Without saying a word, Hazen and Bierce rode back to the head of their brigade and awaited the word to advance. Bierce, who knew well his commander, mentor and friend, later wrote, "Only by a look which I knew how to read did he betray his sense of the criminal blunder."[147]

Howard made his final preparations. He sent clear orders to McLean to place his brigade "in full view of the enemy's works, a little to the right of the point of attack, with a view to attract the enemy's attention and draw his fire." Clearly, Howard intended McLean to expose himself at the edge of the large wheat field in front of Govan to attract his attention enough to mitigate the flanking fire on Wood.[148]

Wood soon rode up to Howard again. It was a little before 5:00 p.m. "Are the orders still to attack?" he asked. Howard's reply was a single word: "Attack!"[149]

Brandley had understood exactly what was coming. He scrambled back up the hill, and while Howard was taking care of the final details, he informed his fellow NCOs of the news. They didn't have to wait long. "Fix bayonets! Charge bayonets! Forward—double-quick—March!"[150]

The blue line surged forward.

Chapter 10

Along the Dead-Line

General Cleburne was aware of the Federal troops massing opposite Govan, but when Kelly's cavalry pickets reported the presence of even more troops off to his right, he knew he had to act. He immediately sent a courier to General Granbury with orders to extend the division's line past Key's two howitzers. The courier found Granbury under a large oak tree. Acknowledging the order, Granbury rose to his feet. Without bothering to relay the order through the regimental colonels, he thundered in a booming voice that carried the length of his command, "Attention, brigade!" Immediately the men rose to their feet, fell in and came to attention. "Right face! Forward! Double quick, March!" And the men were off at the run.[151]

Unknown to either side, it was a race to get into position. Granbury's men ran down Pickett's Mill Road the length of the brigade. When the last regiment cleared the 6th & 7th Arkansas, the brigade halted and faced to the left. The command came down the line to put their percussion caps on their rifles, getting them ready to fire. They then moved a few dozen yards into the woods so they could be on the crest of the ridge overlooking the ravine. About thirty yards in front of them was a slight ledge, beyond which the ground sloped sharply down into the narrow valley. Most likely, the brigade was deployed from left to right: the 7th Texas, 10th Texas, 24th & 25th Texas and the 17th & 18th Texas. The 6th & 15th Texas was definitely stationed at the far right of the brigade and therefore at the far end of the Confederate line. Some of the men had time to throw up a meager barricade using the fence along Pickett's Mill Road and nearby deadfall, but most did not. A small gap still existed between the left of Govan's Brigade and the right of Granbury's. Govan sent the small 3rd Confederate regiment, reduced in size to a two-company battalion numbering less than two hundred men, to fill the gap. To the left, Kelly's Cavalry Division extended the line to the creek but was spread so thin that it was only as strong as a skirmish line. A thin screen of Kelly's skirmishers still covered Granbury's front. [152]

Hazen's brigade began its advance down a smaller ravine that fed into the main ravine from the north. The right half of the brigade generally moved along the western slope, while the left half followed the bottom and eastern slope. The open woods that Hazen's men began their advance in quickly turned into tangled underbrush the farther they went into the ravine. The skirmishers out front soon ran into their Confederate counterparts. One young confederate cavalryman took aim and fired. The man he hit "cried out in the most pitiful, agonizing tone that I ever heard." The lieutenant next to him railed at him, "Now you have played hell—you shot one of our own men." "It was a Yankee," yelled a sergeant nearby, and the chastised lieutenant ordered the men to open fire. The firefight was not a long one— there were far too many of Hazen's men. The cavalrymen were soon in headlong retreat back toward Granbury. [153]

Back at Hazen's main line, the regiments quickly lost cohesion and became fan-like formations, with the bravest in the lead. They ebbed and flowed, almost like a living thing, intermingling and rendering all military order impossible. The color-bearers kept the battle flags furled in their cases so that the snagging and grasping branches did not shred the silk banners. The brigade's alignment began to unravel almost as soon as they started. The frontline regiments, all from Ohio, kept to the western slope of the feeder ravine and slowly drifted to the right. The following four regiments kept to the bottom and began drifting left. The thick foliage and the desire to press forward prevented anyone from noticing, and Hazen quickly lost control of the brigade. Dismounted, as were all the officers in the brigade, and traveling behind the 6th Indiana at the center of the second line, Hazen failed to notice that his brigade had split. [154]

Captain Lewis's Company B of the 124th Ohio was still on the skirmish line, leading the advance of the frontline regiments. Reaching the northern slope of the ravine, they plunged down the slope and ran to the bottom. The skirmishers of the other regiments followed suit. Soon they had collected themselves at the bottom and started up the opposite slope.

In front of Granbury, the thick underbrush downhill parted to reveal the retreating cavalry skirmishers running up the slope. As they ran through

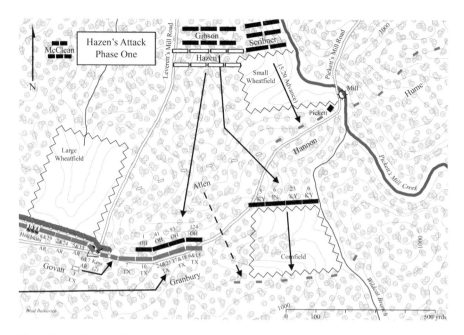

Hazen's opening attack. *Courtesy of the author.*

friendly lines, they warned Granbury's men that "they had better get away from there, as they were coming by the thousand." Rounds began falling among the men. Each regiment threw forward one company as skirmishers. Colonel Franklin C. Wilkes of the 24th & 25th Texas Cavalry sent out Captain Foster and his Company H. After spreading his men out across the front of the regiment, Foster ordered them forward. The right of his company had barely cleared the main line when they ran headlong into Federal skirmishers. Both sides began firing at close range, no more than forty or fifty yards apart. The left of the company continued another seventy-five yards when it could no longer advance. There the two opponents began taking pot shots at each other. The Federals advanced slowly, dashing from tree to tree until some were only thirty to forty feet from Foster's men. Foster then received orders to retreat, and none too soon. In the small encounter, he had already lost two men killed instantly and another mortally wounded. Shot through the bowels, the wounded man was carried back up the hill, where he died the next morning. Casualties were similar in the other skirmish companies from the other regiments. The 6th & 15th Texas lost five men wounded. Private Osceola P. Scott of the 17th & 18th Texas almost didn't make it back. Forgotten on the skirmish line, he didn't realize he was all alone until the Federals were only thirty yards away. Beating a hasty retreat, he had to run over a hundred yards through a shower of bullets to safety. The Federals crept closer and began trading shots with Granbury's main line.[155]

Behind the Union skirmishers, Hazen's frontline regiments crested the opposite slope of the ravine and with a yell ran to the bottom. There they paused to quickly dress their lines and tried to restore some semblance of formation. Colonel Payne, commanding the battalion with the 93rd and 124th Ohio, sent a message to Captain Lewis to force the skirmish line well to the front. Lewis sent word back that they were already engaging the enemy's main line, which was not more than a hundred feet away. With another yell, the regiments surged out of the bottom and began climbing. When the mass of men reached the skirmishers, they absorbed them into the line and continued forward at the run.[156]

The Texans were waiting for them. When the Ohioans reached and passed the ledge thirty yards in front of them, the Confederates leveled their rifles. On command, a sheet of flame and thunder burst forth toward the Yanks, sending thousands of lead missiles their way. Scores of attackers fell in an instant, mostly those in the front ranks. Some of the Federals got as close as fifteen yards before they were spotted. The color-bearers unfurled their flags, those lagging behind caught up and the Federals returned fire. Occasionally a color-bearer would fall, and a flag would tumble to the ground only to be picked up immediately and waved anew. After the first few volleys, the remaining Federals fell to the ground and returned fire from behind trees, rocks or whatever cover they could find.[157]

Frustrated from weeks of attacking a fortified enemy, the sight of the Rebel line standing toe to toe with them in the woods was too much for some of the Ohioans. The cry, "Ah! Damn you! We have caught you without your logs now!" could be heard. Here and there, a single soldier or small groups would rush forward only to be gunned down before they could reach the Rebel line. Between the two antagonists there existed a dead space, a no man's land that no living person could cross. Bierce wrote of this space:

> In many instances which have come under my observation, when hostile lines of infantry engage at close range and the assailants afterward retire, there was a "dead-line" beyond which no man advanced but to fall. Not a soul of them ever reached the enemy's front to be bayoneted or captured. It was a matter of the difference of three or four paces—too small a distance to affect the accuracy of aim. In these affairs, no aim is taken at individual antagonists; the soldier delivers his fire at the thickest mass in his front.

The fire is, of course, as deadly at twenty paces as at fifteen; at fifteen as at ten. Nevertheless, there is the "dead-line," with its well-defined edge of corpses—those of the bravest. Where both lines are fighting without cover—as in a charge met by a counter-charge—each has its "dead-line," and between the two is a clear space—neutral ground, devoid of dead, for the living cannot reach it to fall there.

I observed this phenomenon at Pickett's Mill. Standing at the right of the line I had an unobstructed view of the narrow, open space across which the two lines fought. It was dim with smoke but not greatly obscured: the smoke rose and spread in sheets among the branches of the trees. Most of our men fought kneeling as they fired, many of them behind trees, stones and whatever cover they could get, but there were considerable groups that stood. Occasionally one of these groups, which had endured the storm of missiles for moments without perceptible reduction, would push forward, moved by a common despair, and wholly detach itself from the line. In a second every man of the group would be down. There had been no visible movement of the enemy, no audible change in the awful, even roar of the firing—yet all were down. Frequently the dim figure of an individual soldier would be seen to spring away from his comrades, advancing alone toward that fateful interspace with leveled bayonet. He got no farther than the farthest of his predecessors.[158]

Lieutenant Sebron Sneed of the 6th & 15th Texas noticed a similar phenomenon, if conveyed a little less eloquently. He wrote, "They came up bravely, but our men kept such a shower of minnies in their faces that flesh and blood could not stand it. Again and again they attempted to charge us and approached their line within ten paces of ours, but with shouts and volleys they were forced to retire. The balls flew as thick as hail and death stalked around."[159]

The Confederate artillery did not remain idle, as Key's section of twelve-pounders soon added its voice to the din. With each discharge, they sent solid iron balls crashing through the trees at the ravine, snapping tree limbs and trunks alike, as well as human flesh and bone if it found its mark. If they couldn't see the target, they would fire shells down the ravine or into the woods. Each shell was fitted with a fuse timed to explode after traveling a certain distance, sending jagged iron fragments in every direction. At the close-combat range at the head of the ravine, they undoubtedly used canister, a tin container filled with forty-eight one-inch round balls. The container exploded after leaving the muzzle, effectively turning any cannon into large shotgun. Each blast left a cone of destruction in its wake, shredding men and foliage

The Ravine, photographed in winter for a clearer picture. The 1st and 41st Ohio charged up this slope from right to left. *Author's collection.*

alike. Over at the large wheat field, Swett's ten-pounder Parrott rifles opened fire. While no enemy was in their direct line of sight at the moment, they knew where the Federals had assembled beyond the field and threw exploding shells in the area, hoping to hit anyone unlucky enough to be in the way.

In the ranks of the 41st Ohio, a sergeant noticed something white thrust up among the Rebels, calling out to his comrades that it was a white flag. The regiment sprang to its feet and charged, but the Texans met them with a withering blast of musketry. Those Ohioans not killed or wounded dove to the ground or fell back the few feet to their original line.[160]

Major John R. Kennard walked along the line encouraging his men with his usual refrain, "Put your trust in God, men. For He is with us." However, he couldn't resist a taunt at the enemy, and took up the cry "Come on—we are demoralized!" Almost immediately, a Union ball struck him in the head, and he fell. It was a glancing blow, serious but not life threatening. Raising himself up, Kennard exclaimed, "Boys, I told them a lie—and I believe that is the reason I got shot."[161]

With the 124th Ohio blasting away at the enemy and his company intermixed with the rest of the regiment, Captain Lewis made his way to the left of the line to see the battle progressing there. The left of the regiment rested on Pickett's Mill Road, and the road ran up a small hill toward the 6th & 15th Texas. At the edge of the road, Lewis met up with Lieutenant Charles M. Steadman from his company. Standing face to face with Lewis and with his back to the enemy, Steadman informed Lewis that one of the best men in their company, Adam Waters, had been killed. Steadman also told him that a great many others had been badly wounded. "Captain, we can hold this position until reinforcements come up, can we not?" asked Steadman. "I think so," replied Lewis, "but what we want is to carry this hill."

No sooner had Lewis spoken the words than a great stream of blood sprouted from Steadman's left breast. The wounded man gave Lewis a look as if to say "My time has come" and then fell dead into Lewis's arms. The captain moved the body away from the road and gently folded the man's arms across his breast. He took Steadman's watch and memorandum book and laid his saber across the body. Leaving his friend's body, he moved back to the right, where he came upon Captain John B. Irving of Company C. Irving was sitting with his back against a small tree, smoking his pipe, and his face was ashen. Lewis asked the man if he was wounded, and Irving replied, "Yes, it is all day with me." Irving also told Lewis that the regiment's lieutenant colonel was wounded, as was another fellow company commander. The 124th was suffering terribly.[162]

Back at the right of the line, the 1st and 41st Ohio faced a new threat. While the Ohioans were pinned down by the Rebels to their front, Key's howitzers and the 6th & 7th Arkansas fired down the length of the ravine and into their flank. Confederate skirmishers advanced to get closer, but fire from the 1st Ohio forced them back to their lines. Still, it was only a matter of time before they tried again. Lieutenant Colonel Kimberly knew he had to get help. He sent back the 1st Ohio's adjutant, Lieutenant Homan, but he was shot down before going a hundred yards. A second officer was sent, hopefully with better results. How could the right of the brigade be taking such devastating fire from the flank? Where was McLean?[163]

General McLean's task was to appear before the large wheat field and make his presence known. He didn't have to have his men assault the works across the field, merely engage Govan and prevent him from dispatching troops to the left. His presence in front of Govan could also have split the fire of Key's howitzers between the ravine and the field, although since Cleburne put one section at the head of the ravine specifically to fire down it, that might

Pickett's Mill Road looking west. Lieutenant Charles M. Steadman of the 124th Ohio was wounded near the bottom of the hill. *Author's collection.*

not have occurred anyway. Regardless of where Key may or may not have focused his fire, McLean was supposed to try and divert it, and he did not. His men never left their assembly area to the right of Wood's division. This left Govan free to shift men wherever he needed them to support Granbury, and Hotchkiss free to direct the fire of his artillery wherever he thought it would do the most good. Still, not all of McLean's men were idle. He had a skirmish line connecting Howard's forces with the rest of the Twenty-Third Corps back at Mount Tabor Church Road. They kept some pressure on Hindman's Division, as well as Polk's and Govan's Brigades. One of them wounded a lieutenant from the 1st Arkansas who was manning the rifle pits in front of Polk's Brigade. His comrades brought him back behind the main line, where he urged his fellow Arkansans to become Christians. Sending for the commander of the regiment, Lieutenant Colonel William H. Martin, the junior officer told him he was a wicked man and that he must lead a better life. The men of his company tried to comfort him by telling him how many Yankees he had killed. "Yes," he replied, "I killed three. But my brother, don't gloat over it. Do your duty, but don't gloat over it." Dying men speak with no fear of reprisal. He passed away shortly after sending home a few loving messages.[164]

William Smith spent the early afternoon in relative quiet, finding time to read the May 25 edition of the *Atlanta Appeal*. He had finished reading Anna H. Drury's *Misrepresentation*, which he thought was very good, and also found time to send his copy of the *Appeal* up to General Polk. Soon, however, events overtook him and he was on his way to the frontlines. There he spent the battle hauling crates of ammunition, under fire, to the men of his brigade at the breastworks.[165]

The situation among the frontline Ohio regiments was getting critical. Colonel Kimberly sent another messenger to find Hazen or anyone of authority to bring up the second line, but the messenger was unable to find anyone. Colonel Payne sent a similar messenger, but still the second line did not come to their aid. The reason, of course, was because the second line was no longer behind the first and therefore couldn't come to their support. The only troops behind them were the divisions of Wood and Johnson, and help from them was not forthcoming, at least for the moment. The second line had drifted to the left. So while the Ohio regiments were being slammed to a halt by close-range volleys from Granbury's men, the two battalions of Indiana and Kentucky boys were moving up the ridge beside them in the face of Kelly's dismounted cavalry. It was a decidedly one-sided contest. Dismounted cavalry rarely go toe to toe with infantry—their carbines lack the range to counter rifle fire, and slugging it out with infantry isn't in their job description anyway. Plus, the numbers were on Hazen's side. Whereas the second line of the brigade may have had eight hundred to one thousand men, Kelly probably had that many, maybe a little more, on his entire line, and he had to cover the eight hundred yards from Granbury to the creek. The Federals easily pushed the cavalry up and over the ridge, at which point the Rebel cavalrymen fled across a small cornfield to the other side.[166]

The Union men were ideally suited to turn the Confederate flank. They were abreast of the flank of the 6th & 15th Texas. At the end of Granbury's line, a spur branched off from the main ridge to the south and afterward turned directly east, paralleling the main ridge. In front of Hazen's men, another smaller spur branched off the main ridge and ran southeast. Between the two spurs was a fifteen-acre cornfield enclosed by a fence. The north end of the field continued more or less level for about twenty yard before sloping downward into a small hollow and then up again to the opposite fence. In the hollow at the middle of the field was a small strip of woods, and to the left was Wildcat Branch, a small stream that fed into Pickett's Mill Creek. Across the stream was a commanding hill. To the right were open woods and the unprotected Confederate line. However, before the Federals could turn to the right and roll up the enemy's flank, they would have to deal with the cavalrymen on the other side of the cornfield. Already they could be seen tearing down the fence on their side and using it to make more barricades. If they turned right without eliminating the threat, they would be enfiladed in turn.

General Granbury saw the threat to his flank and immediately sent to Govan for help. With no action to his front, Govan felt free to pull Colonel George F. Baucum's 8th & 19th Arkansas and Semple's battery of four Napoleons out of the line and to Granbury's assistance. Granbury sent his adjutant general, Captain Joseph T. Hearne, to lead the regiment where it was needed most. They sprinted down Pickett's Mill Road and the new trails into position behind the 6th & 15th Texas and to the west of the cornfield. Cleburne, from his headquarters immediately behind the 6th & 7th Arkansas, was also busy rushing reinforcements to his flank. He ordered Mark Lowrey and his brigade to Granbury's assistance and appealed to Hood for help as well. Lowrey pulled his men from behind Tucker's Brigade of Hindman's Division and moved them at the double-quick toward Granbury. Cleburne met Lowrey en route and told him to move rapidly. He explained the tactical situation to Lowrey, and as he hastily left for other parts of the field, he ordered his subordinate to "secure Granbury's right." As they ran down the new trails they encountered Baucum's men ahead of them. Lowrey hurried them off to Granbury's right.[167]

Unaware of the growing Confederate presence behind Granbury, Hazen's second line crossed the first small draw, reached the northern end of the cornfield, climbed the fence and scrambled down the slope of the field into the wooded hollow below. General Hazen watched from behind a tree at the top of the hill. Dozens of men fell as the cavalrymen opened up from the other side in an attempt to slow them down. The 5th Kentucky stopped in the woods in the hollow, but the 6th Indiana and 23rd Kentucky to their left kept going up the opposite hill toward the Rebels. The left of the 23rd rested on the fence along Wildcat Branch. The 6th Kentucky fell behind the 23rd and refused the line to the east. Confederates, probably more cavalry skirmishers from Kelly's Division, had occupied the hill across the stream and poured a flanking fire into the brigade as it crossed the cornfield. The 6th Indiana and 23rd Kentucky stopped short of the barricade and engaged in a firefight with the Confederates on the other side.[168]

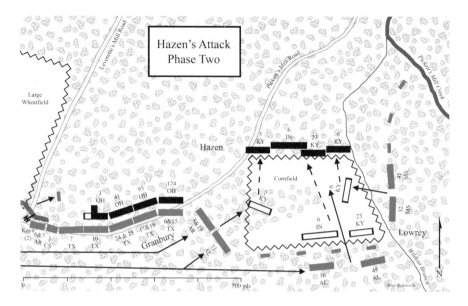

Hazen's second line attempts to outflank Cleburne's position. *Courtesy of the author.*

Sergeant Brandley was fighting for his life. With a rush, the 23rd Kentucky and 6th Indiana closed in on the fence, and the two sides fought each other through the fence and over the barricade. The pressure on the cavalrymen was too great, however, and they fell back a short distance into the woods but kept up their fire. Brandley loaded and fired his rifle so fast that the barrel became too hot to touch. A bullet ricocheted off a rock and struck him near the instep of one of his feet. It wasn't a serious wound. At first, the pain made him dance, but then it made him mad—mad enough to forget about the hot gun barrel and continue firing. Suddenly, a ball struck his rifle near the lower band and smashed it flat. Undeterred, he picked up another from a dead comrade and continued fighting.[169]

Captain Charles C. Briant, from Company K, 6th Indiana, was also in the thick of the fighting. When the 5th Kentucky failed to move forward from the hollow behind them, it left the fence to the right of the 6th in Confederate hands and exposed their flank. Captain Samuel F. McKeehan, acting major for the regiment, ordered Briant to run back to the 5th and tell its colonel to charge up the hill and take the fence in front of them. Briant took off immediately, but as soon as he cleared the end of his own line, the Confederates at the fence fired at him. One bullet grazed his back, not deep enough to seriously wound him but with enough force to send him somersaulting down the hill. After "going through some other gymnastic performances," as he put it, he landed on his feet and reached the hollow. There he found Colonel William W. Berry of the 5th and delivered the message.[170]

Unfortunately, Colonel Berry was having problems of his own. The 8th & 19th Arkansas had advanced, running into the 5th Kentucky in the hollow. Taken by surprise in the flank, the Kentuckians were fighting back as best they could. To compound the problem, Lowrey's Brigade was coming on line. General Lowrey decided against deploying his brigade out of its march column first and then advancing. Instead, as soon as the lead regiment, the 33rd Alabama under Colonel Samuel Adams, cleared the 8th & 19th Arkansas to its front, it turned to the left deployed on line beside the Arkansans. Each successive regiment in Lowrey's Brigade did the same after clearing the unit to its front.[171]

Captain Briant sprinted back up the hill to the 6th Indiana. The first thing he found upon his return was the prostrated form of Captain McKeehan. Briant knelt down to help the man, but McKeehan grabbed his coat collar and pulled him closer. He had been shot through the mouth, and though it was difficult to speak, the wounded captain told Briant to never mind him and look after the men. Briant laid the man back down and stood up to face the enemy. What he saw beyond the fence was Lowrey's Brigade deploying in the woods ahead of them. Concerned for the safety of the line, he ran behind the two regiments to the extreme left of the 23rd.[172] There Sergeant Brandley was fighting it out with a few die-hard Rebels near the fence at the corner of the field. Taking a squad of men, he rushed the enemy and "saw enough there to make my blood run cold; plenty of dead men, with a very lively line behind them." It was Lowrey's Brigade. Brandley and company fired into them, and the Confederates returned the favor, killing a number of the Kentuckians. Brandley notified his company commander of the danger, and the captain looked off to the flank with his binoculars. A round smashed into the captain's knee, spinning him around on one leg. However, the captain maintained his balance and nonchalantly put the glass back up to his eyes for another look. The Confederates were extending their line down to Wildcat Branch and working their way into the hollow to their left and rear, behind the 6th Kentucky.[173]

Events took a turn for the worse in front of the 5th Kentucky. General Kelly, the former colonel of the 8th Arkansas, came upon the 8th & 19th and, with Colonel Baucum and Captain Hearne, led it in a charge against the Kentuckians. The 33rd Alabama charged with them. It was too much for the Kentuckians, who broke and ran back up the hill. The Arkansans and Alabamians followed into the open field, but the 33rd split. The seven left companies kept to the Arkansans, but the four right companies veered to the right and remained in the wooded hollow. The Kentuckian's flight was short-lived. They rallied at the fence on the northern border of the field and fired into the advancing Confederates, killing Captain Hearne as he entered the cornfield. The Rebels halted and returned the fire. Lowrey's right regiments passed the cornfield and engaged Scribner's brigade on the ridge above the Pickett house. But lacking cover in the open field, they soon decided to retire back into the woods. The 8th & 19th Arkansas formed on the right of the 6th & 15th Texas of Granbury's Brigade, and the 33rd Alabama kept contact with the 8th & 19th. General Lowrey helped rally the 33rd, personally riding among them on his favorite horse, Rebel. Once in position, the two sides settled into a firefight. There was no room for Semple's Napoleons to deploy, and the battery spent the rest of the battle idling behind the lines.[174]

A few of the right companies of the 6th & 15th Texas from Granbury's Brigade also joined in the charge against the 5th Kentucky, taking a few prisoners. The regiment was getting low on ammunition, and Lieutenant Sneed was using a large butcher knife to cut the cartridge box off a wounded man so he could redistribute the cartridges to others. He had just finished when a member of his company brought one of the new prisoners to him. Sneed ran up to the Federal, his knife upraised in order to cut off his cartridge box. The poor Yankee came to the obvious conclusion that this butcher knife–wielding Confederate meant to kill him. He threw up his hands and gave the lieutenant "the most pitiful face." Sneed could not help himself, and amidst the violence and chaos around him, he burst into laughter.[175]

Captain Briant made it to the left of the 23rd Kentucky's position and also saw Lowrey's men moving into the hollow behind them. On his own initiative, he gave the order to leave. Yelling "Retreat!" at the top of his lungs, he ran the length of the two Union regiments. Sergeant Brandley saw and heard Briant as he ran by, and soon other officers were giving the same command. It was just as well, as the two regiments had just about exhausted their ammunition, and the Rebels surrounded them on three sides. Flight was the only realistic option to avoid capture.[176]

With the enemy on three sides, the three Federal regiments ran a gauntlet of fire on their way to safety. In addition, the right regiments of Lowrey's Brigade charged and pursued the fleeing Yankees. Confusion was everywhere. About ten men from the 6th Indiana were captured during the flight, not counting those left killed and wounded on the field. A Rebel colonel rode ahead of his men and into the ranks of the retreating 23rd Kentucky and ordered it to halt and form their ranks. Needless to say, the Kentuckians demurred. But they also left the colonel unhurt. On the way back, Brandley came upon his company's second sergeant, William Johnson. "Brandley, don't let the Rebels get me," he implored. Even though Johnson had given him a hard time earlier in the war, Brandley couldn't leave the wounded man alone.[177] "Where are you wounded," Brandley asked. "Cross your fingers, put your hands under my head, and lift me up stiff-legged," said Johnson. Brandley did as directed, and Johnson threw his arm around his neck. Together they gingerly made their way down the hillside. Confederates passed around them but unaccountably left the two men alone. Brandley put the wounded man down once they reached the bottom of the hollow. There he examined Johnson's injuries. All the fingers except the thumb and index finger on one of Johnson's hands had been shot off. A flesh wound ran above one thigh, and another ball passed through his side, from left to right, above his hips. It was a miracle they had gotten as far as they did. Brandley enlisted another man in their company, Ed Buehl, to help him. Together they tried carrying Johnson in a blanket, but the man screamed in pain. They needed a stretcher. Leaving Buehl with Johnson, Brandley left the woods and ran the gauntlet of fire back to the first fence.[178]

The three Union regiments halted at the fence alongside the 5th Kentucky, turned around and "fired with great execution upon the enemy advancing across the cornfield," according to Hazen, who had remained along the fence near the center of his brigade. Hazen noted, "The enemy came on in fine style, coming up from the ravine beyond; but after one volley from our men along the fence they were out of sight, to a man, in twenty seconds." Lowrey's men retreated and took cover behind Kelly's old barricade on the other side of the field. There the two sides fired at each other at will. The Union regiments were undoubtedly intermingled along the fence line. Sergeant McDermott of the 23rd was lying down behind the fence and firing at the Confederates when a Confederate bullet struck his right thigh. The round went clear through his leg and hit a soldier from the 6th Kentucky in the head, killing him.[179]

Some of Cleburne's staff officers, observing the withdrawal of the 8th & 19th Arkansas and the 33rd Alabama on the brigade right, thought the line was broken. In fact, the two regiments reformed shortly thereafter, with Baucum's men next to the 6th & 15th Texas and the Alabamans to their right. However, the staff officers ordered up reinforcement to fill the supposed gap. These reinforcements came in the form of Quarles's Brigade. General Hood,

Northwest corner of the cornfield looking east. The modern cornfield is half the size it was during the battle, when it extended farther to the east. *Author's collection.*

responding to Cleburne's earlier request for help, had dispatched Quarles and his men to the Irishman's assistance. They had just arrived and were now marching to the far right to help avoid a disaster. General Lowrey also came to the same mistaken conclusion as Cleburne's staffers and hurried his two rightmost regiments, the 32nd and 45th Mississippi, from the right of the brigade line to the left. When they arrived, they found Baucum and Adams reformed and the line stabilized. The new arrivals formed behind them in support. Without anywhere else for them to go, Cleburne formed Quarles's men behind Lowrey as a second line. In reality, there actually was still a gap in the line but not a break. A small interval existed between the right of the 33rd Alabama and the rest of Lowrey's Brigade because when Baucum and Adams fell back, they moved more to the left relative to where they started their charge in order to connect with Granbury.[180]

The situation on the left of Hazen's brigade had stabilized for the time being, but the Ohioans on the right were still getting mauled in their close-range firefight with Granbury. General McLean and his men failed to advance and cover the right flank of the brigade. Colonel Scribner and his brigade were supposed to move forward and protect Hazen's left. They weren't there to prevent Lowrey outflanking the Union regiments in the cornfield. Where were they?

Chapter 11

Tell Mother I Am in the Front Ranks Yet

Colonel Scribner was late, but it wasn't his fault, at least not initially. General Johnson had ordered Scribner to deploy the men in his brigade on the left of Gibson's, the second brigade in Wood's divisional column. As the colonel understood it, when Wood's division advanced, Scribner would move forward. If any Confederates tried to flank Hazen's lead brigade, Scribner, a hundred or so yards behind him and to the left, would be in a position to strike the enemy in the flank in turn. Nowhere in Scribner's post-battle report or in his memoirs does he refer to the intention to move forward alongside Hazen. In fact, it would seem Scribner believed Wood's entire division would attack at the same time since he mentions protecting the flank of the division and not just the lead brigade. Even more curiously, Scribner also fails to mention whether or not the rest of Johnson's division was supposed to follow him.[181]

Scribner's lead units in front of the small wheat field were already taking casualties. The first casualty in Company A of the 78th Pennsylvania was James Little. As his company commander held him, Little requested, "Tell mother I am in the front ranks yet." He repeated it three times before passing away in the arms of the regimental chaplain.[182]

When Hazen finally advanced at around 5:00 p.m., there was space for Scribner's brigade to shake out into line of battle, but there was still only enough room for two regiments in the frontline. The 37th Indiana and the 78th Pennsylvania took the assignment. The left of the 37th rested on Pickett's Mill Creek, while the 78th deployed to their right. Howard sent a messenger at about 5:15 p.m. prompting Johnson to begin the advance. He responded that "he was sending one up," which probably meant that Scribner hadn't even started. Scribner himself wrote that he began moving forward at 5:00 p.m., but it was probably closer to 5:30.[183]

The 78th Pennsylvania fired a volley from the north fence of the wheat field into the Rebels on the opposite ridge, the same ridge where five hundred yards to the southwest, Hazen's men were fighting for their lives. Then the brigade rushed down the slope into the field. Each man of the 78th carried a fence rail with him. The Confederates fired into them, and stray shells from Key's howitzers, fired from the far right, exploded among them. The 37th jumped across the small stream at the bottom and entered the woods on the other side. After they passed the mill and Pickett residence, they ascended the ridge. They too picked up logs and debris and carried them along. Kelly's cavalrymen, crouching down in their rifle pits near the summit, greeted them with a blistering volley. However, they didn't remain long in the face of such overwhelming odds and quickly beat a hasty retreat. The 37th crested the ridge and fell prone on the summit overlooking Wildcat Branch. Hume's men on the ridge on the other side of Pickett's Mill Creek fired into their left, causing several casualties. To their right, the 78th also pushed back the cavalrymen to their front. Once they reached the summit, the Pennsylvanians dumped their rails into a barricade and returned fire. The men lay on the military crest, and the officers and file closers behind them were dangerously exposed along the summit. Scribner's men, instead of taking a cue from Hazen and pursuing the thin line of cavalry skirmishers, hunkered down into a firefight.[184]

While advancing, John J. Kirk of the 37th had picked up a rotten-looking log several inches in width and about five feet in length. Beside him, John Q.A. Withrow criticized him for doing so. "You will be glad to get your head behind this log before long," replied Kirk. Sure enough, as soon as the firing started, Withrow ended up beside Kirk, using the log for cover and as a rest for their rifles. "You made fun of me for carrying this chunk, and just as I said, you are the first man to get behind it," said Kirk. Suddenly, Kirk jumped up, his face covered with blood. A minié ball had passed through the rotten log and struck his head. The wound was not fatal, but Kirk headed for the rear, leaving his rifle behind. Withrow's rifle soon became unusable, and he picked up Kirk's discarded one and continued firing.[185]

While practical and understandable given their experience charging breastworks the past three weeks, the lack of aggressive spirit Scribner's men demonstrated by carrying their own cover into battle doomed Hazen's fight for control of the cornfield. If Hazen had forced back approximately half of Kelly's men to the west, then no more than four to five hundred cavalry skirmishers faced Scribner across Wildcat Branch, not including Hume's men across the creek. Scribner probably had at least four, if not five times that many on hand, though with only two regiments in front the odds may have been even. Still, rarely could a line of cavalry skirmishers stand up to an aggressive charge by infantry in line of battle. Scribner appeared more concerned with the flanking fire from Hume's men across the creek than moving forward and protecting Hazen.

Lieutenant Colonel William D. Ward of the 37th Indiana was complaining loudly about Hume's men and the trouble they were giving him. First, Ward sent Major Thomas V. Kimble to Scribner expressing his concerns about his open left flank. Kimble returned with assurances from the brigade commander that it would be taken care of. Shortly after the major's return, the Confederate skirmishers apparently made an advance against both the 37th and 78th, an audacious move given the disparity in numbers. But by this time, the cornfield to Scribner's right front was full of Lowrey's men chasing Hazen's second line back across the field. This allowed Wheeler, who was present and coordinating the two cavalry divisions, to have Kelly concentrate his men against Scribner. The dismounted Rebel cavalry advanced in skirmish order and, according to the 78th Pennsylvania's historian, "did not have any very definite line of battle, but they seemed to be in countless numbers, and they did not waver until, at some points, in front of the 78th Regiment they were not ten paces from our line." A few of Lowrey's regiments, in a disordered mass, passed the cornfield and joined the rush. Hume's men across Pickett's Mill Creek added their fire to the assault, and some of Kelly's men may have crossed the creek to help them. This prompted Ward to send his adjutant to Scribner with the dire warning that his left flank was being "assailed." Before the adjutant returned, the Confederates advanced again. A minié ball struck Ward in the cheek, forcing him out of action. Command fell to Major Kimble.[186]

Concerned about the threat to his left, Scribner decided to secure that flank of his brigade. He ordered three of his regiments across the creek, leaving only the 74th Ohio to support the 37th Indiana and the 78th Pennsylvania. The 38th Indiana crossed first, sprinting across the mill dam. As soon as they were over the creek, the nearby cavalry skirmishers greeted them with a volley. Luckily, the Confederates fired too high, and none of the Federals were wounded. The 38th deployed into line, followed by the 1st Wisconsin to the left and the 21st Ohio at the far end. When all three regiments were ready, they rushed up the hill. Humes's cavalry retreated before them, and the Federals took control of the ridge across the creek. Casualties were light. The 38th lost only two men wounded, and casualties in the other two regiments were probably similar. Scribner now had his brigade in a secure position with a single, unbroken line of battle, with only the 74th Ohio in reserve. Skirmishers from the 37th and 78th took up positions in Wildcat Branch ravine. They were still about a hundred yards behind and to the left of the fence on the northern side of the cornfield and too late to help Hazen's men. Except for a few stragglers, Hazen was already gone.[187]

The four Ohio frontline regiments on Hazen's right continued to get the worst of it. On the far right, a Confederate regiment again tried to form across the flank of the 1st Ohio, but again the Federal rifle fire forced them back into their works. Wounded men along the entire line crawled back down into the ravine seeking whatever shelter they could behind rock outcroppings in the streambed. Colonels Payne and Kimberly both dispatched several messengers asking for support, but they returned empty-handed or did not return at all.[188]

The men of Hazen's brigade had suffered enough, and their commander knew it. While not yet sunset, the woods were beginning to get dark due to the low angle of the sun and the smoke from thousands of rifles. Whereas Hazen's battalion commanders were busy sending messengers looking for him (or anybody else in authority for that matter), Hazen himself was sending messengers to Wood asking that the rest of the division advance and continue the attack. No help was forthcoming. Finally, after forty-five minutes of sustained combat at close range, Hazen commanded the left wing to retire. In small and large groups, they made their way back down into the ravine, and from there back to their starting point. However, many stayed behind. Captain Briant remembered that the 6th Indiana stayed along the fence all night, although as subsequent events showed, that was probably not the case. Still, a good portion of them may have stayed until well past nightfall. Hazen's adjutant, Lieutenant James N. Clark, ordered Captain Isaac N. Johnston and his 6th Kentucky to retire. Enough Union men remained along the fence to continue firing and keep up the appearance that it was still manned.[189]

Falling back was no easy matter for the brigade right. Neither of the two battalion commanders received orders to retire. When the 93rd Ohio saw the left of the brigade heading toward the rear, they went with them on their own. Companies I and B of the 124th Ohio went with them. The rest of the 124th remained on the line fighting, and Colonel Payne stayed with them.

Over on the far right, the Confederates made yet another attempt to turn the flank of the 1st Ohio, causing the regiment to pull back at right angles to the 41st Ohio. The 1st Ohio counterattacked and retook their lines, but the pressure was just too great. Colonel Kimberly ordered the two regiments of his battalion to fall back on his own volition. The retreat was orderly except for the three right companies of the 1st, which the Confederates pressed heavily as they retreated and nearly surrounded them. They regrouped at the bottom of the ravine, marched down to the feeder ravine, turned left and made their way back up to their original assembly point. The fact that Granbury did not immediately counterattack and capture all the wounded weighs heavily to the fact that, like the fence at the cornfield, enough Federals remained behind, wounded or otherwise, to give the appearance of an unbroken line. Most of the 124th Ohio, for example, remained in close-range combat with the Texans.[190]

As Hazen and his men made their way back up the feeder draw, they encountered a large body of Union troops marching south toward them. It was Gibson's First Brigade, headed toward the big ravine. Their relief was on the way, thirty minutes too late to do any good.

Chapter 12

In the Thickest of the Fray

As Hazen and Scribner's men withered under the fire from the hard-fighting Confederates, the rest of Howard's men cooled their heels at the jump-off point. They could hear the violent sounds of battle up ahead. Shells from Swett's Parrotts crashed through the woods, exploding over and among the men waiting their turn to enter the maelstrom. One shell wounded several men in Company C of the 15th Ohio.[191]

Once back among friends, the remnants of Hazen's Second Brigade did their best to piece themselves back into recognizable units. One portion of the 93rd Ohio rallied around a lieutenant and went off searching for the rest of the regiment. They met a remounted Hazen in company with Howard, also on horseback, along Leverett's Mill Road. The lieutenant approached Hazen, saluted him and said, "General, where is our brigade? We wish to report to our regiments?" Tears began to roll down Hazen's cheek. "Brigade, hell," he answered. "I have none. But what is left is over there in the woods." He then kindly addressed the Ohioans and bade them get all the rest they could.[192]

General Wood was aware of Hazen's repulse and lack of progress, so at least some of the latter's messengers made it to the division commander. Finally, after the Second Brigade had been fighting for about an hour, Wood ordered Gibson's First Brigade forward. In Wood's report and writings decades afterward, he explained that the First Brigade was to first relieve the Second and take its place. Then, having secured the advance position, they would charge the Confederates. Since Hazen's men would be screening their approach, they would not have to worry about moving enemy skirmishers out of the way or being the object of direct fire until they were on line with Hazen. With Gibson starting the charge so close to the Confederates, Wood hoped it would have a greater chance of success.

Why did Wood wait so long to send in Gibson? Why not have the entire division attack in one large column as many, such as Hazen, thought would happen? Neither Wood nor Howard provided an explanation. After the battle, Wood merely stated that he was ordered to attack. Of course, Hazen and Bierce remember the exchange about sending their brigade in alone differently. Howard was silent on the matter, referring only to Wood's inquiry whether or not to attack. The two men said even less about the delay between Hazen's assault and Gibson's advance. Wood wrote in his report only that he ordered Gibson to advance and relieve Hazen, with no explanation for the delay, and incidentally, with no mention of having Knefler follow.[193]

The two lines of the brigade started forward, but like Hazen before them, order immediately degenerated into chaos. The three front regiments—from left to right the 32nd Indiana, 15th Wisconsin and 89th Illinois—apparently guided on the north–south feeder ravine and drifted to the left. They too found the going rough, and the neat lines of advancing infantry soon became mobs. Hazen met them as they made their way down the feeder ravine, and described the 32nd Indiana as "the first regiment I saw coming to my support, did so in detached fragments, and not as a regiment." Soon the three regiments reached the northern crest of the large ravine and beheld the scene before them. Across from them, just below the opposite crest, the remnants of Hazen's brigade were still furiously engaging Granbury's Texans. Below them, the wounded and skulkers crowded the slopes and bottom of the gorge. With a yell, the line ran down the slope. Granbury's men greeted them with a withering fire of musketry, and Key's guns let loose shot and canister into their right flank. Upon reaching the bottom, the line cheered once more and charged up the hill.[194]

The 32nd Indiana hit Granbury just to the right of the 124th Ohio, which was still on the slope battling it out with the Texans. According to William Oliphant of the 6th & 15th Texas, they

> pressed steadily forward until they were almost upon us, but they could not stand our terrible fire. When but a few feet from the points of our bayonets, they seemed to wither away, and those not killed or wounded were forced to fall back. The color-bearer of the regiment fell with his colors, instantly another seized the flag and held it aloft only to fall dead. Again and again it was raised until six brave men yielded their lives in trying to keep it flying.

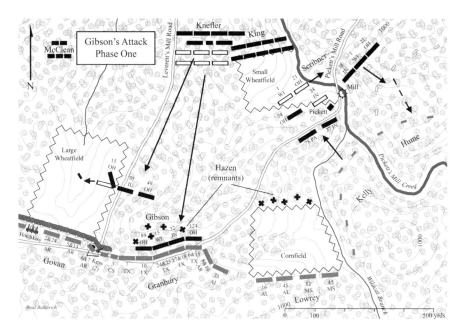

Gibson's brigade joins the fight. *Courtesy of the author.*

> *The sixth man fell with the flag in front of our company only about ten or twelve feet from us. There it lay within our grasp. I could have reached it with a single bound but thought as it was already ours, I would wait until their line had been completely driven back before picking it up.*

Perhaps Oliphant instinctively knew that if he crossed Bierce's dead-line to grab the flag, he too would end up as one of the many prone forms dotting the forest floor that late May afternoon. A few of the 32nd did make it to the Rebel works, but they were all quickly captured or killed.[195]

The 15th Wisconsin and 89th Illinois to their right fared little better. The 15th charged over the remnants of the Second Brigade and into the Texans. Some got within ten feet of the Confederates before they fell. The remainder of the regiment fell prone about fifteen yards from the Rebels and joined Hazen's men in returning fire. Likewise, the 89th advanced to within twenty-five yards of the Rebel works before the Texans opened fire. According to the regiment's lieutenant colonel, "here the fire was so murderous that the column paused, wavered, and sought such shelter as they could find." The right of the 89th didn't extend into the bowl at the head of the ravine, leaving a large gap between the end of the regiment and Key's two-gun battery posted there.[196]

Sergeant Isaac K. Young of the 89th Illinois wrote in a letter to his hometown newspaper that as the regiments approached the Texans, the Rebels "exhibited white flags over their works and shouted to our boys not to shoot, they would surrender." As the Federals drew near, the Confederates sprang to their guns and poured volley after volley into them. Either the Rebels resorted to subterfuge and abused the white flag on multiple occasions or otherwise brave Union men felt the need to resort to an excuse as to why they could not carry the position. However, at least three regiments from two different brigades mentioned the ruse, so there may be a kernel of truth to the anecdotes.[197]

The second line of the brigade—from left to right the 49th Ohio, 35th Illinois and the 15th Ohio—advanced along Leverett's Mill Road. The right of the 35th Illinois and the left of the 15th Ohio rested on the road. As the line advanced, the right of the 15th Ohio entered the long wheat field, exposing them to Govan's men on the other side. They were still out of killing range of the infantry's rifles, but Swett's battery switched from firing blindly into the woods to taking direct aim at visible targets. Company C seemed to attract shells that day, and Swett's first shell exploded above them, wounding Lieutenant Thomas C. Davis and a number of the color guard. The second line of the brigade came to a halt before reaching the ravine, theoretically to support the first line. This left half of the 15th exposed in the middle of the field. Govan's infantry opened fire, and rounds from the fight up ahead flew thick in what Sergeant Major Andrew Gleason called a "galling cross-fire of musketry and artillery." There were no units to the right of the 15th, and Lieutenant Colonel Frank Askew feared an attack from that direction. He threw Company A out to the right in a skirmish line. The left of the regiment, in the woods, was only slightly less safe. Gleason took cover behind a convenient log during the halt.[198]

Colonel Gibson actively encouraged his men. Isaac Young of the 89th described him as being "in the thickest of the fray," so he probably showed himself among the frontline, at least at the beginning of the brigade assault. He also apparently toured the second line as well, for when he saw the position of the 15th Ohio, he ordered the entire regiment to refuse to the left in order to protect the flank of the whole brigade. The regiment attempted to comply but "were thrown into dire confusion by conflicting or misunderstood orders of our regimental commander, Colonel Wallace."[199]

With the three front regiments stalled, Gibson needed to regain forward momentum, so he ordered the second line to charge. Up came the men at

The large wheat field looking north from the position of Brigadier General Daniel Govan's Brigade. *Author's collection.*

the double quick. As they crested the ridge at the northern edge of the ravine, Key's howitzers met them with a blast of canister. Iron balls ripped through flesh and shredded the ranks. Down the slope they went into the ravine, and with a yell scaled the boulders and trees of the opposite side. The 414 men of the 49th Ohio charged through the prone forms of Hazen's men and the 89th Illinois to within ten paces of the Texans' barricades. Most were exhausted by the charge and fell to the ground alongside those who had tried previously to brave the storm of lead. The bravest few continued forward. Francis A. Kiene of Company I "got so near that the smoke of the Rebel guns curled up against me." When he looked around, he saw only one other man from his regiment besides himself in the advance. The rest were dead. With the pragmatism of a veteran, he retreated to the main line and threw himself to the forest floor where he could hardly distinguish the living from the dead. 1st Lieutenant Francis R. Stewart of Company A found cover behind a tree when he was not gathering cartridges from the dead and wounded to redistribute to the men. The tree was good protection from the front but was naturally exposed to fire from the sides, especially the right, from which oblique fire pelted the men. He later wrote, "Surely, God guided the missiles, or many more of us would have been killed. I felt bullets go between my head and my ears, and they passed through my hat and my hair."[200]

The 35th Illinois, on the right of the 49th Ohio, either passed through the prone 89th Illinois with the 49th or struck the Confederates on their own without passing through the first line. The 15th Ohio had to deal with more than just the Confederates. They were still trying to sort out the disorder caused by the attempt to refuse the regiment when the order came for the second line to charge. Bugler William S. Iler sounded the advance before the officers could sort out the confusion and get the men back in formation. In a strange quirk, the right of the regiment had bent so far back that when the order came to charge, it somehow reoriented itself to the front and took a position on the left of the colors. This had the practical effect of switching the two halves of the regiment. The 15th charged into the woods, more in a mass of men than a line of battle.[201]

They charged down into the amphitheatre at the head of the ravine and up the other side. Key's howitzers tore into them as they advanced, and Granbury's infantry to the right of the 15th added their rifle fire to the carnage. Up they ascended until they were within a few feet of the Confederates. There the attack stalled, just as the others had before them. Color Sergeant Ambrose Norton was killed in front of the works, dropping the regiment's colors. The Texans shot down five more of the color guard as they attempted to pick up and hold the flags aloft. Eventually, they fell near the works and lay there unattended. Unable to go forward, the men of the 15th hugged the ground and took shelter wherever they could. Not every injury in the charge was a result of enemy fire, however. Colonel Wallace tripped over a rock on the way down into the ravine and fell to the ground hard, wrenching his back. This left the 15th under the command of Lieutenant Colonel Askew for the remainder of the evening, though Askew was unaware of his commander's injury until afterward.[202]

Sergeant Gleason noticed two men taking shelter behind the same medium-sized tree ahead of him. When a ball struck one of them in the hand and he headed toward the rear, Gleason crept up and took his place. The other fellow wasn't lying flat against the ground, but he wasn't firing his rifle either. Suddenly, Gleason heard the unfortunate and familiar "splat," in his words, of a bullet striking flesh and bone. A ball had entered the temple of the man lying to his left, killing him instantly and covering Gleason in blood and brains. The poor man did not move, and Gleason would not have

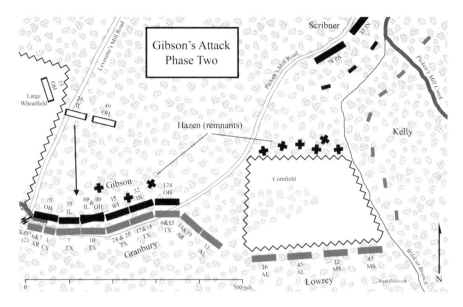

Gibson's second line moves forward and assaults Granbury's Texans. *Courtesy of the author.*

known he was dead if not for the sound of the impact and the gore sprayed all over him. Gleason quietly crept away and found another vantage point from which to view his charges.[203]

The crossfire from the left and the right devastated the regiment. Captain Cyrus Askew of Gibson's staff was present, and Lieutenant Cope implored him to go to the rear, report the state of the regiment and the crossfire and send support to the left and right to take the pressure off. Captain Askew declined to leave but suggested Cope go instead. Cope took the assignment and made his way back down into the ravine, where he met Captain Joseph R. Updegrove of Company H. Updegrove's face and neck were covered in blood from a wound behind his ear. Cope suggested he go to the rear, but Updegrove wouldn't leave his men. Cope sent for somebody to relieve Updegrove and continued on his way. As he ascended the slope on the opposite side of the ravine, "it seemed almost impossible to escape the bullets and shells of the enemy. The minnie balls seemed thick as hornets about a nest which had been suddenly disturbed, and a shell seemed to explode near him almost every step." He made it up the slope unscathed and continued toward the rear.[204]

In the woods beyond the ravine, Cope encountered Colonel Gibson and General Wood. They were both "laboring under terrible stress of excitement."

He tried to explain to them the condition at the front. Just then, General Howard rode up. Seeing the adjutant, he asked Cope directly about the situation. Cope reported the events as best he could, and Howard replied, "Go back and tell the men that I will have troops sent in both on their right and left as soon as I can get them." Cope started back but had gone just a few steps when a shell exploded above the group of officers. As the adjutant watched, Howard's horse whirled around. Howard, shielding his eyes with his sleeveless arm, exclaimed, "I am afraid to look down! I am afraid to look down!" Cope examined the wound and informed the general that a fragment had struck his boot. In fact, the shard of metal had penetrated the sole, gone through the leather and badly bruised the bottom of his foot. It was a painful but not debilitating wound. Cope started back toward the front. He made it back into the ravine and up the other side but ended up behind the 15th Wisconsin. He slowly made his way back to the right, looking for the 15th Ohio, but by that time, it was beginning to get dark.[205]

All along the line, Gibson's men hugged the earth and tried to survive the maelstrom above them. Francis Kiene with the 49th Ohio crept up behind three dead men for shelter. A soldier in front of him was killed by a ball entering his shoulder. If the ball hadn't struck him, it would have struck Kiene. To stand up was foolish and suicidal. Second Lieutenant William F. Gibbs rose and bellowed that there was another line of their own men ahead and that they should stop firing. Within seconds, he fell dead. Many Federals along the line huddled under the Confederate barricades right beneath the muzzles of the Confederates. In many instances, this was safer than being a dozen or more yards farther back with the main line. The Confederates were shooting over their heads at the greater threat. In fact, Lieutenant Cope observed that this fire "did little damage to the men closest to the enemy's line in our immediate front but was killing the wounded who were lying in the ravine and on its slopes to our rear."[206]

Over on the far left, the men of the 32nd Indiana had given all they had but could not budge the 6th & 15th Texas from their barricades. For the last time, the Union men fell back, and Private Oliphant was sure the fallen flag before him was as good as theirs. But just as the last of the Yankees retreated to the crest, one of them turned and noticed the flag lying on the ground. Oliphant watched in amazement as he dropped his rifle, ran back to the fallen colors and picked them up. Then, in an amazing act of defiance, he boldly straightened himself up to his full height, gritted his teeth and proudly waved the Union banner in the Texans' faces. Every rifle within sight was instantly leveled at the man, but one of the Texans cried out, "Don't shoot him—he's too brave." In an amazing act of chivalry, the men lowered their rifles, and scores of throats broke out into a lusty cheer. The lucky man ran back to his lines with the flag amidst the accolades of his enemy. There, the man fell in among his prone comrades on the slope, and the fighting continued anew.[207]

Gibson's brigade had been engaged for about an hour. It was approaching 7:00 p.m., and the sun was low in the trees. True sunset was only about thirty minutes away, but the forest was already dark under the leaf canopy. The second assault on the Confederate lines had obviously failed. Most knew it much sooner than that. All along the lines, the buglers sounded the recall. Lieutenant Colonel Askew remembers the brigade bugler giving the order around 6:00 p.m., whereas Sergeant Gleason thought it was closer to dusk. Regardless, most were unable to comply. The men were simply too close to the enemy barricades to safely fall back. Any movement would have triggered a volley, and if the Confederates sensed a retreat, possibly a violent counterattack. Most prayed for darkness and the opportunity to crawl back unseen. Unknown to Gibson's men, help was on the way, but like Hazen before them, it would be too late.[208]

Chapter 13

Canister Rattled Like Hail

The soldiers in Knefler's Third Brigade waited their turn to enter the fight. Hotchkiss's artillery continued to shell the woods, and rounds fired too high by the Confederates landed among them. In the 79th Indiana, one man from Company A was killed by a minié ball while the regiment stood in line awaiting the order to advance. Several others were wounded.[209]

General Wood knew the battle was over after the repulse of his first two brigades, and circumstances beyond the battlefield contributed to the end of the fighting. At little before 6:00 p.m., a messenger arrived from General Thomas. He found Howard sitting among the wounded, nursing his injured foot and dictating the battle from there. The courier carried new orders from Thomas, who wanted Howard to "connect his right with General Schofield's left and to take up a strong position which he could hold until he can be re-enforced, and if necessary to do this our left must be refused; that he must not place his troops in such a position as to risk being turned, and to say to General Johnson that he must place his troops so as to secure our left flank." In essence, Thomas wanted Howard to take up a defensive position until he could send reinforcements to Howard and reestablish direct contact between the two isolated divisions and the main army.[210]

Accordingly, Wood decided to send Knefler forward, but his orders were different from the previous advances. As Wood put it, Knefler was "simply ordered to relieve the First Brigade and hold the ground without renewing the assault. The purpose of holding the ground was to cover bringing off the dead and wounded." His men were to add their strength and firepower to those already on the firing line, but there would be no assault across the dead-line. The reinforcements would engage in suppressive fire, keeping the Confederates' heads down while others brought as many of the wounded as possible back to friendly lines.[211]

The men of the Third Brigade got ready. Lieutenant Woodcock of the 9th Kentucky watched and waited. He observed the remnants and wounded from Hazen and Gibson's commands drift back into friendly lines "in great disorder." Wood ordered Knefler to leave the 86th Indiana behind to cover Leverett's Mill Road and the flank of the brigade. This left the 59th Ohio, 13th Ohio and 17th Kentucky in the frontline. The second line remained the 19th Ohio, 79th Indiana and 9th Kentucky.[212]

At Knefler's command, the men stepped off. Unfortunately, the dense vegetation and challenging terrain caused the frontline to split. The 59th and 13th Ohio continued almost due south. They came up the south slope of the ravine to the right of the 124th Ohio, still engaging Granbury's Texans since the first assault. Major Joseph T. Snider, commanding the 13th Ohio, later wrote, "Our advance had to be made over ground most unfavorable. Dense woods, tangled vines, rocks and ravines impeded our way at every step, but we pushed on under a murderous fire, never halting for a moment until within about twenty yards of the crest of the ridge, when we found ourselves under a formidable line of defenses from which the enemy poured a deadly of musketry and artillery." There, just at the crest of the ravine, they lay prone and added their firepower to the remnants of Hazen and Gibson's commands.[213]

The officers of the 89th Illinois and 49th Ohio didn't get the message that Knefler was only there to relieve and support them. The 49th's Lieutenant Colonel Samuel F. Gray urged his men to renew the assault with the new line. Unfortunately, (or fortunately in light of the futility of previous attempts) the men were so exhausted that only a few rose to the call to charge the Rebel barricades. Francis Kiene was one of them. He advanced a few paces in front of the Union line and fired at some Texans who were taking cover behind a large log. Kneeling down to reload, he was drawing the ramrod from his rifle when two balls struck him. One passed through the collar of his coat, the other struck his left elbow. The arm fell uselessly to his side, and Kiene made his way back to cover. Only one other person who had advanced with him returned to safety.[214]

The 17th Kentucky drifted farther to the left. In fact, its commander, Colonel Alexander M. Stout, had a hard time keeping order in the regiment. Rounds began dropping among them, and shells from Key's howitzers up

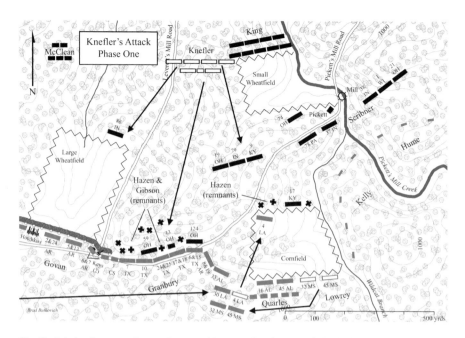

Knefler's brigade moves forward to provide cover for the rest of the division. *Courtesy of the author.*

the ravine began falling among them long before they came within sight of the enemy. The noise made it almost impossible for the troops to hear commands from their officers, and the bushes and sapling made it even more difficult to carry them out. Eventually, the regiment made its way up to the fence along the northern border of the cornfield. Its left rested about fifty yards from the Wildcat Branch ravine. The 17th immediately engaged the Confederates to their front and left.

Kelly's men in particular, located on the hill across the branch, posed a problem for the 17th. They subjected the Federals to an oblique and flank fire. Help was nearby. Scribner's men were to Stout's left and rear. The 78th Pennsylvania and 37th Indiana were at the top of the ridge behind them, and their skirmishers were in the ravine with the 17th. But according to Stout, the Pennsylvanian's skirmish line did not line up with the left of the Kentuckians. This exposed the left of the 17th to flanking fire from the Rebel cavalrymen, who were also engaging Scribner to the front. Obviously, this concerned Colonel Stout a great deal, and he made his way over to the Pennsylvanian regiment to confer with its commanding officer, Colonel William Sirwell. Sirwell refused to advance his skirmishers to link up with the 17th. Going over Sirwell's head, Stout sought out and found Scribner and pleaded his case. Unfortunately, Scribner also refused to properly link the two brigades. Stout would have to make the best of a bad situation. Still, the Kentuckian's arrival was fortuitous, for they were not the only reinforcements entering the fray at the cornfield.[215]

The 4th Louisiana of Quarles's Brigade found itself opposite the gap between the 33rd Alabama and the rest of Lowrey's Brigade on the Confederate frontline. Unlike the other regiments of the brigade, it had seen action in large pitched battles like Shiloh and Baton Rouge. It had also never been surrendered or exchanged during its service. Seeing the gap and the Federals beyond, its commanding officer, Colonel Samuel E. Hunter, ordered the regiment forward. Through the gap they went. When the regiment cleared the gap and Colonel Hunter saw the Federals on the other side of the field, he ordered a charge. According to James Martson, the men "advanced slowly across a strip of woods about 200 yards in length. We came to the edge of an old [corn] field. We were ordered to charge when we raise a yell and rushed forward, driving the enemy before us." Up the slope they went toward the Federals at the top. Colonel Hunter stopped to help a wounded corporal, and the regiment left him behind. The two sides collided at the fence, and a hand-to-hand struggle ensued. Eighteen-year-old Simon Alcide Landry rushed ahead of the line and into the Yankees. A Union lieutenant stumbled and held up his hands but was still holding his revolver. Another Confederate next to Landry shot him. A terrified Federal turned to flee before Arthur Blanchard, and the Louisianan thrust his bayonet into his back. The blade snapped off while imbedded in the dead man. General Quarles, who had followed the regiment out into the field, realized that the Louisianans were alone and unsupported. He ordered them to fall back across the field and into the woods. They retreated down the hill, reformed in the gap in the line and settled down into a shooting match with the Yankees.[216]

The Louisianans were helped on their way back by the timely arrival of the 9th Kentucky. The 17th Kentucky had been taking fire from the Confederates in the cornfield, as well as Kelly's skirmishers posted on the hill on the other side of the Wildcat Branch. Colonel Stout called for help, and Knefler ordered the second line of the brigade forward. The first regiment to arrive was the 9th Kentucky, followed quickly by the 79th Indiana and the 19th Ohio. Lieutenant Woodcock wrote, "The two lines of our brigade were soon merged into one. We commenced pouring a continual volley of balls into the enemy's ranks that soon caused him to stop and take some consideration for his own safety, and soon afterward to fall back a short

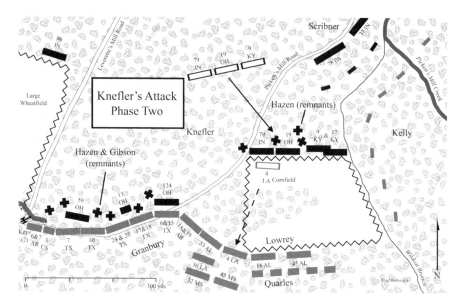

Knefler's brigade secures the cornfield. *Courtesy of the author.*

distance for the cover of the timber." Despite Woodcock's account, it's just as likely that Quarles ordered the 4th Louisiana to retire just as Knefler's second line arrived and hurried them on their way.[217]

When the 9th Kentucky arrived, the 17th Kentucky shifted left. It ended up in the ravine itself, and the two regiments became intermixed. When the 19th and 79th arrived, they picked up the fence rails from the edge of the field and moved them about twenty yards into the field. There they threw the rails down to make a slight barricade at the edge of the shelf where the field began to slope downward into the wooded hollow. Lying prone, both regiments, along with the 9th and 17th Kentucky to their left, kept up a brisk fire with Lowrey and Kelly's men as the sun set and darkness began to fall.[218]

On the far right, the 86th Indiana, though detached from the brigade, was not idle. It advanced to the northern edge of the large wheat field, essentially doing the job McLean's brigade was supposed to do, while the Twenty-Third Corps men remained idle to the rear. Govan's men opened up on them with long-range musketry fire, and Hotchkiss trained his battalion's gun tubes on them as well. With an obvious flair for the dramatic, the unit history related:

> *Shells shrieked and burst all around…solid shot tore the limbs from trees overhead, which fell with a crash threatening to crush the men and added*

to the horrid din. Grape-shot and canister rattled like hail about and whipped the underbrush and shrubs like a hurricane, but the Eighty-sixth never flinched.

At some point, a shell fragment struck the metal scabbard holding Colonel George F. Dick's sword, shattering it and badly wounding him. He had to be carried from the field. The regiment endured the bombardment until darkness fell and night gave them cover from the Confederate gunners.[219]

Night did not bring an end to the fighting everywhere along the line. In the cornfield, the two sides blazed away at each other, aiming at the muzzle flashes from the other side of the field. Lieutenant Woodcock was standing behind the lines talking with a fellow officer when, near sunset, a ball struck him in the right thigh, penetrated about an inch of flesh and bounced out again. The ball did not tear his pants, but it did stuff them into the wound. Thinking the injury minor, Woodcock pulled the cloth out of the wound. Only then did it begin bleeding. He fell back a few yards and vomited behind a tree. Afterward, feeling no other ill effects, he went back to the firing line and rejoined the fight. Gradually, the Union regiments slowed their fire. They began running low on ammunition, with just enough remaining to repulse a feint by the Rebels but not a full charge.[220]

In the ravine, however, the fighting tapered off a bit more with the coming of night. Captain Foster of the 24th & 25th Texas remembered that the firing gradually slackened after nightfall and ceased altogether when it became completely dark. Captain Lewis of the 124th Ohio wrote that the firing ceased along the line after dark. The fighting had ended, but the battle was not over. The two sides were, in some cases, merely yards apart. The Federals had to begin the process of disengaging from the enemy and falling back to the shelter of their jumping-off point, and the Confederates were just as eager to make them pay before they could.[221]

Chapter 14

By God, It's the Rebel Forward

By nightfall, the Union offensive along Pickett's Mill Creek had come to a halt, a failure. The Union commanders threw four brigades into piecemeal battle against an equal number of Confederate brigades. But the Confederates occupied commanding terrain, and the results would be predictable. Now, night and darkness gave the promise of salvation to thousands of Union soldiers, some literally trapped under the barrels of the enemy.

On the far right of the Union line, Colonel Askew detailed parties from the 15th Ohio to collect the wounded and escort them to the rear. When they finished, the colonel ordered the regiment to withdraw—at least, that's the dry, official version, but the reality was far from being that simple. For example, despite his search, Adjutant Cope failed to find the 15th on the ridge and fell back after dark only to rejoin the regiment where it rallied near a house close to the assembly point. Sergeant Gleason's experience was likewise confusing and lonely. From his vantage point, he could see no one. Smoke clung to the woods, and nobody was visible. Although the bugle kept sounding the recall, Gleason thought it best to stay put and await developments, especially since Confederate bullets continued to sweep the ground around him "like a hailstorm." After dark, a man from Company I came limping past Gleason. He was grievously wounded in the thigh and asked Gleason for help. The sergeant took the wounded man's blanket roll in one hand and held him up with the other. Together they made their way down to the bottom of the ravine, where they met the 15th Ohio's Major McClenahan, along with a bugler, who was still sounding the recall at intervals. After relating what meager information he had, the two continued on. Gleason escorted the wounded man about a mile to the rear and then rejoined the 15th where it was assembling behind the lines.[222]

To the left, the 49th Ohio maintained its position until dark, at which point they helped as many wounded as they could back to the main line. Francis Kiene was one of them. With one arm useless, he dropped his rifle after retiring a short distance into the ravine. He examined his arm and only then did he realize he had been shot. Not feeling any pain when struck, his first thought was that something had hit him and merely numbed the arm. Only now, when he had time to examine himself, did he discover blood streaming down his side. Still, he did not feel uneasy, and he began his way to the rear under his own power, passing other wounded along the way. When he made it back to the main line, he discovered that they were digging in and building entrenchments of their own. These men were most likely from King's brigade, which had come up behind Scribner and began digging in along the northern edge of the small wheat field. Realizing he would no longer see combat, Kiene discarded his cartridge box, keeping its brass plate as a memento, and continued rearward in search of a field hospital.[223]

The 89th Ohio employed a slightly different tactic while withdrawing. First, it retired a short distance to the rear after nightfall. Exactly how far isn't clear. The regiment's report merely states they "withdrew beyond range," which could mean to the shelter at the bottom of the ravine or closer to the assembly point in the north–south feeder draw. Either way, only when most of the regiment was out of immediate danger did their colonel detail men to go back and remove the wounded. After the details left to carry out their task, the 89th withdrew the rest of the way into the Federal lines.[224]

The 32nd Indiana must have withdrawn at about the same time, but not before Private Oliphant of the 6th & 15th Texas captured a young prisoner, about his own age. During their brief conversation in the field, Oliphant learned that the two had shared the same bench in primary school in Lawrenceburg, Indiana, and that the colonel of the Yank's regiment was a name Oliphant's mother had often mentioned as a childhood friend in her youth. The coincidences didn't end there. After the war, Oliphant learned that his aunt, still living in Lawrenceburg, had made the flag of the 32nd and presented it to the regiment—the very same flag that a brave young Northern soldier had saved right before their eyes. In addition, May 27 was his mother's birthday. War is full of such improbable coincidences.[225]

In the 6th & 15th Texas, opposite the 124th Ohio, the command came down the line to cease fire. The Ohioans below them heard the order and rose up. The Texans ordered them to surrender, and a few of those closest to the Confederate lines did, but the Federals used the end of the shooting and the darkness to reorganize. One Union officer, possibly as a bluff, shouted, "Run over them, men!" This elicited a volley from the Texans, and the Federals withdrew to the bottom of the ravine. Captain Lewis of the 124th remembered that his regiment, which had gallantly stood its ground and maintained its position from the first volley, was "withdrawn from the field in squads and without any word of command that all could hear." Still, in the confusion, there were plenty of Federals who remained on the ridge above the ravine. The 13th and 59th Ohio from Knefler's brigade, with positive orders to remain and give the other units time to bring off their wounded, stayed where they were on the slope. Many others from the wreckage of Hazen and Gibson's commands also remained behind. Either they did not notice in the darkness and smoke that only the dead and wounded remained; they mistook Knefler's men for their own units, not realizing they had already left; or fear made them unwilling to retreat.[226]

The situation was a little more organized in the cornfield, if no less desperate. There the regiments of Knefler's brigade at least had a contiguous line along the fence and behind the barricades the 19th Ohio and 79th Indiana had advanced to the brow of the hill. Still, ammunition was low, and the shooting fell to a lull after nightfall. Colonel Stout reported that individual soldiers would inform him that they were out before slipping away in the darkness. Undoubtedly, there were many who didn't bother with the informing part and just left. Individuals made attempts to carry the wounded to the rear, as it was impossible for wagons or ambulances to advance through the terrain. The officers of the 9th Kentucky assigned details to remove the injured. Lieutenant Woodcock listened to many of the wounded who lay trapped between the two lines. They wailed their "prayers and lamentations," and many asked to be shot. Woodcock's fellow Kentuckians helped those they could. It then became a waiting game to see whether the Union could withdraw completely in the darkness before the Confederates reacted.[227]

Hiram Granbury was one Confederate who didn't want to wait. Reports of enemy movement so close to his front certainly made their way to him. In all probability, he heard them himself. Even General Cleburne in his report stated that the enemy was "so near it [Granbury's line] that their footsteps could be distinctly heard," although whether he also heard that for himself is unknown. The possibilities were dire. The Federals could have been using the darkness to move reinforcements forward and form them prior to an attack. If that was the case (and with the two lines being so close), there would be little to no warning if fresh brigades of Union soldiers suddenly surged out of the darkness. The thin Confederate lines would be overwhelmed. Even if the only threat remaining in the darkness before them was a disorganized enemy, the chance to bag a few prisoners and possibly push the enemy back a safe distance was too tempting to ignore. Granbury sent one of his staff officers to Cleburne asking for permission to attack. Likewise, Govan sent Captain Bostick on a similar errand.[228]

More Confederate reinforcements arrived. A brigade commanded by Brigadier General Edward C. Walthall from Hindman's Division arrived behind Cleburne's men near nightfall. Walthall was a solid and dependable brigadier who would soon rise to division command. His three Mississippi regiments, the 24th & 27th, 29th & 30th and 34th, filed in along the low ground behind Cleburne's Division and awaited orders. There is also evidence that some of them relieved Granbury's exhausted Texans and fired a few volleys into the Federals. Their presence surely helped Cleburne's peace of mind and probably gave him the latitude he needed to consider a limited counteroffensive. About 9:00 p.m., he ordered Granbury and Lowrey to push forward skirmishers to feel out the enemy. Cleburne recorded no such orders for Govan, possibly because the works on his front were strong and the threat posed by the Federals on the other side of the field limited.[229]

The Texans did their best to comply, but with the Federals so close to their front, the deployment of skirmishers was difficult and precarious. Granbury probably had thoughts of charging regardless of what he found, because his orders, to Colonel Wilkes of the 24th & 25th Texas at least, were to "charge in the woods at the sound of the bugle." The colonel sent his adjutant to Captain Foster with orders to deploy his Company H as skirmishers again in front of the regiment, from left to right. This Foster did, posting one man every eight or ten feet and about ten feet in front of the main line. As they did so, they took a number of prisoners—Union soldiers who had crawled or gone to ground only a short distance from the Rebs but deemed it too dangerous to try and crawl back. Once deployed, the Texans waited in the darkness for the bugle call that would send them out into the unknown. They could hear the Yanks in front of them move by the rustling of the leaves and deadfall. They could also hear them whispering. The tension was nerve-racking. Foster admitted honestly that, "To make that charge in the dark and go in front at that; and knowing that the enemy was just in front of us was the most trying time I experienced during the whole war."[230]

While the Confederates made their preparations to charge, the Union soldiers continued gathering their wounded. Sergeant Brandley of the 23rd

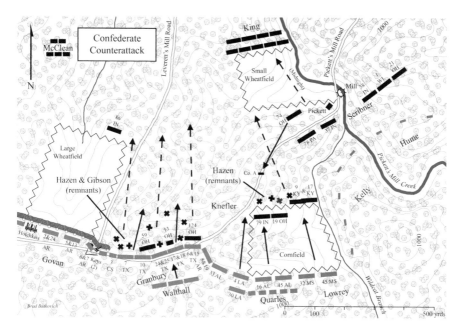

Cleburne's Division launches a night attack, pushing back Wood's division to its starting point. *Courtesy of the author.*

Kentucky continued his search for somebody that could help him move Sergeant Johnson, who he had left in the wooded hollow in the middle of the cornfield. As fortune would have it, he soon came upon a large man carrying a pair of stretchers

"You are the very man I want," said Brandley. "Come with me to a wounded comrade who must be saved." "Where do you belong?" the man answered. But he quickly thought better of the question and declined to help, stating, "I belong to the 49th Ohio and am now on my way to carry a wounded officer of my regiment from the field." Brandley insisted, even going so far as to lie, stating that Johnson was also an officer. And when he offered to assist the man in retrieving his wounded officer from the 49th Ohio in exchange for his help, the man relented. The two crossed the fence at the northern end of the cornfield and made their way down into the hollow, shots landing among them as they went. There they found Johnson and Buehl where Brandley had left them. Using a stretcher, the three men carried Johnson back to their own lines. They found a makeshift aid station near where Brandley had filled his canteen and overheard the officers discussing the upcoming attack. With Johnson now safe, Brandley offered to keep his part of the bargain and help retrieve the officer. The other man declined and departed into the night, leaving Brandley to care for Johnson.[231]

Though he was safely behind the Union lines with the rest of the 124th Ohio as it reorganized, Captain Lewis felt apprehensive about leaving the body of his friend, Lieutenant Steadman, so near the enemy. He asked one of his sergeants, Orson Vanderhoef, if he would find two other volunteers to help him retrieve the body. According to Lewis, Vanderhoef was "made of the best of stuff," and he readily agreed, finding two others who would also venture into the dark unknown. Together, the four passed out of the lines and made their way through the ravine and back to the 124th's previous position along Pickett's Mill Road. It was a surreal journey. Dead pine trees had been set alight by bursting shells, which "cast a weird and gloomy light" along their path. When they reached their destination, the wounded that had been left behind began begging for help. Some wanted water. Others asked to be carried back to avoid capture. The four kept to the task at hand and found the lieutenant's body where Lewis had left it. Unfortunately, the lieutenant's saber was gone. They searched for it, but their efforts were in vain.[232]

Meanwhile, at the top of the hill, Cleburne was coming to a decision. Granbury was complaining that his skirmishers could not advance with the Federals so close to his lines. With the two choices being to wait for the Yankees to make the first move, which could also mean lying in the dark all night with them so close, or charging to drive them off, the decision for a man of Cleburne's temperament was easy. He gave Granbury his consent to charge his line forward.[233]

Along Granbury's line, a single bugle sounded the charge. Captain Lewis and his three companions had just picked up the body of Lieutenant Steadman when they heard "the silvery notes of a bugle, so clear and soft one might have mistaken it for some night bird's call."

"Captain, what's that?" asked Sergeant Vanderhoef.

"I guess that is some artillery call," said Lewis. "It is certainly not an infantry call."

Vanderhoef finally recognized the notes. "By God, it's the Rebel forward. I've heard it many a time on picket, and we'd better be getting out of here pretty God damned quick."

No sooner had the words left his lips than a Texan skirmisher stepped out into the road and fired at the group. Lewis ordered the group to separate, and the four escaped into the night.[234]

A primal, guttural roar erupted from their lips as the Texans leapt forward. Captain Foster called it a "regular Texas Yell or an Indian Yell, or perhaps both together." The Confederates fired as soon as they began. The Federals responded in kind, lighting up the wood "like a flash of lighting." The commander of the 13th Ohio reported that his men fired their last round of ammunition. However, the abruptness of the charge and the close proximity of the two lines proved too much for the Federals along the slope of the ravine. They broke, many of them throwing down their guns as they ran. The Texans were soon among them, and the lines intermingled in a confused melee in the dark, lit intermittently by the flash of a musket. One of Foster's skirmishers got so close that a Federal soldier grabbed him and told him to "fall in quick, as Company C was already gone." The Texan complied—for about twenty paces. He then hid behind a tree and waited for his companions to catch up. Sometimes the Confederates would find five to twenty Federals behind a fallen tree. "Don't shoot, don't shoot," they would plead.[235]

At the bottom of the ravine, confusion reigned. Foster's company found scores of wounded and surrendering Yankees along the banks of the stream. Without a doubt, other regiments did too. Some of the Texans accidently fought each other in the darkness, but no fatalities were reported, at least not publicly. To Lieutenant Collins of the 6th & 15th Texas, challenges rang out in the inky blackness up and down the gorge. "Who's that?" "Who are you?" Occasionally, the report of a musket would reverberate along the slopes. If the reply was, "I belong to the 167 New York, or 144 Illinois," then a Texan would command, "Well, come into my shuck, ye greasy flitter." Collins thought they captured about two hundred Federals in that way. Charles A. Leuschner of the 6th & 15th Texas recalled that they were less charitable when they discovered Yankees in their midst:

> *They would sometime be so mixt up that they could not tell wich was a Rebel or wich was the yankey's; and they would ask what regiment do you belong to, and sometimes the answer would be the 40th, and our boy's knew that we dit not have no 40th regt. in our brigade; and, therefore, they would Kill such. Sometimes the answer would be the 24th; and when they would ask the 24 What, 'the 24 Ohio,' and they were servt the same.*[236]

As soon as Granbury's men advanced, Walthall's men moved up and took their place behind the improved breastworks. Over at the cornfield, Lowrey's Alabamians charged across the field and into the Union line a little after Granbury's Texans. Cleburne's report did not mention that Lowrey also attacked, but the Louisianans of the 4th Louisiana did, as did the reports and reminiscences of most of the Union units and soldiers who received them. Lieutenant Colonel Henry G. Stratton of the 19th Ohio reported that the enemy "advanced under the cover of darkness and suddenly charged our lines. We fought him bravely, but being pressed by overwhelming numbers and without support, we were compelled to fall back." Most of Knefler's men agreed that Granbury's men initiated the charge at or near the brigade right. The Federals in the cornfield gave a better account of themselves, firing the last of their ammunition and falling back in much better order than the bedlam that transpired in the ravine. Colonel Stout of the 17th Kentucky recalled, "The enemy, commencing on the right of our brigade, made a furious charge, cheering and yelling. Regiment after regiment fell back until all were in motion." The commander of the 9th Kentucky agreed: "The enemy formed in front of the right of the brigade and, giving a signal with bugle, moved forward intending to gain our rear and capture us. We met them with a volley—the last cartridge—and fell back in good order." Lieutenant Woodcock remembered that the enemy attacked "with a fury that was in our then circumstances, simply irresistible, and therefore, after giving them our last shot, we hastily fell back across the hill."[237]

General Quarles was on hand to personally order the 4th Louisiana to advance. In a clear, sharp voice, he yelled, "Fire and charge!" Forward sprang the Louisianans. They picked up speed as they cleared the brush in the woods and entered the open cornfield. By the dim light of the stars they could see a "perfect sea of glittering bayonets" up ahead. As the Federals fled before them, Lowrey's men, along with Hunter's Louisianans, crested the slope at the northern edge of the cornfield. There they halted, either by orders or by natural inclination. Knefler's men, along with the remaining survivors from Hazen's brigade who had remained behind, took shelter at the bottom of the ravine. Slowly and painstakingly, they found each other in the darkness and made their way north to where King's brigade was digging in.[238]

Knefler's withdrawal left Colonel Scribner in a difficult situation. Half his brigade was still on the east side of Pickett's Mill Creek. The other half remained on the ridge near the Pickett house, overlooking Wildcat Branch. It had been there all evening, and the skirmishers of the 78th Pennsylvania and 37th Indiana, on the southern slope of the ridge, were trading shots with Kelly's cavalry skirmishers across the branch. During lulls in the fighting, Scribner's men had made barricades of their own from nearby fence rails and fallen logs. Ammunition in the brigade was also dangerously low after several hours of fighting. Suddenly, Kelly's skirmishers charged with a yell, in concert with Granbury and Lowrey. A volley from the Federals stopped them in their tracks, but the charge was probably more adrenaline and

"Rebel Yell" than a serious attempt on the part of Kelly's men to breach the lines. It is doubtful few on either side were wounded in the exchange.[239]

What did alarm Colonel Scribner was the mass of retreating soldiers moving past his right flank. He made his way to the end of his line and confronted them. Among them was Colonel Stout, on his way back from the cornfield with his regiment. When Scribner asked him what he was doing, Stout replied that he had been ordered to fall back. "I think you might have had the courtesy to notify your supports of such a movement," retorted Scribner. Colonel Stout merely replied, "I know nothing about it. I am only obeying orders in falling back." Considering Scribner's earlier personal refusal to advance his lines to align with Stout's, the lackluster response of the 17th's exhausted colonel is understandable.[240]

With no more friendly troops on the right, Scribner's flank was open and dangerously exposed. Luckily, the 74th Ohio was still in reserve behind the 78th and 37th. Scribner ordered Colonel Josiah Given to move his regiment to the right and deploy skirmishers to screen the weakness of the line. Given gave the assignment to Captain John W. McMillen and his Company A. The company filed out along the ridge, extending the brigade line, and soon came into contact with Lowrey's Confederates, exchanging shots across the small draw between the main ridgeline and the northern edge of the cornfield. The night was dark, and the Confederates probably had no desire to advance further anyway. The Confederate counterattack ground to a halt, and the Battle of Pickett's Mill was over. Still, the woods were full of wounded men trying to find succor and lost soldiers hoping to reunite with their own regiments. Many, including Scribner's whole brigade, had to find or return to their own lines. Confusion and apprehension were the bywords for the night.[241]

Chapter 15

God Would Have Mercy

Astillness fell over the battlefield. It was broken only by the groans and desperate pleading of the wounded and an occasional gunshot. Colonel Scribner found himself in an uncomfortable position. His brigade was alone and isolated near the Confederate lines, an isolation magnified by the dark stillness. As a precaution, he sent instructions to his three right regiments. If the enemy attacked and the pressure was too much, they were to fall back down the ridge and across the wheat field, pivoting on the 37th Indiana at the creek. The end result would be that the three regiments would end up facing west with their back to the water. With King's men facing south, they would catch any Confederates entering the wheat field in a devastating crossfire.[242]

General Johnson was apparently much more anxious for the safety of his subordinate brigade than Scribner was. The colonel was content to hold his ground for the rest of the night. Johnson, however, became concerned when the stream of retreating soldiers did not include his Third Brigade. He sent a staff officer to investigate the state of affairs on Scribner's front. When he arrived, Scribner described the situation and assured the officer that everything was well. Johnson was not convinced. The staff officer returned and ordered Scribner to have his wounded brought back to King's line and report the progress to him. Scribner relayed the order down to his regimental commanders, but before they could fully comply, the staff officer returned yet again to Scribner. This time, he expressed Johnson's impatience with the delay. At this point, one must wonder why Johnson didn't just visit Scribner in person and coordinate the withdrawal he obviously contemplated. With

King entrenching and Carlin idling behind the lines, he couldn't have been too busy.

Regardless, Scribner assured the staff officer that he was carrying out Johnson's orders. In addition, he explained his contingency plan in which his right regiments would fall back and turn the wheat field into a killing zone. The officer left but returned again shortly. This time, he had preemptory orders from Johnson: Scribner and his brigade were to fall back immediately, even if they had to abandon those on the skirmish line. The colonel wasn't about to do that. He sent for Major Augustus B. Bonnaffon of the 78th Pennsylvania, known for his knack for light infantry tactics, and ordered him to take charge of the brigade skirmishers. Once he saw the balance of the brigade fall back across the wheat field, he was to withdraw the skirmishers by alternating his lines. One group would cover another as they retreated. The retreat began in earnest around midnight and went off without incident. By 2:00 a.m., the brigade was back together on the reverse slope of the hill in rear of King's Regulars.[243]

The Confederates were also busy adjusting their lines during the night. Captain Foster and his company fell in with the rest of the 24th & 25th Texas at the bottom of the ravine after the charge. Colonel Wilkes then ordered the captain to take his company up the southern slope of the ravine and establish a skirmish line on the heights. The rest of the regiment would fall back to their original line and begin converting their hasty barricades into proper earthworks. The other regiments of Granbury's brigade probably issued similar orders, with the balance of the unit falling back to begin entrenching along the evening's line of battle. After some repositioning, Foster had his men stationed just below the top of the hill, on the reverse or inside slope of the ravine, to avoid being seen by any Federals. Soon, Union campfires began to spring up in the distance. To Foster, there seemed to be thousands of them. A runner emerged out of the dark ravine and told the captain that a friendly battery had taken position directly behind them. They were going to shoot over the Texans' heads and drop shells among the illuminated Union camps. This was no easy feat for the artillery technology of the time. Cannoneers had to aim by hand, and there was little to no practical experience with indirect fire. The communication technology simply did not exist to give artillery spotters the ability to relay distance and adjust fire from a forward position. Indirect fire could still be done, but it was largely a matter of guesswork and luck. Add in the darkness and the fact they had to shoot over the heads of a friendly skirmish line, and the task seemed insurmountable. With a loud "boom," the first shell let loose from the mouth of the cannon, sailed over Foster's men and exploded in the middle of the Union camp. The rest of the battery followed, and for an hour, the shelling continued until the Union soldiers wisely extinguished their fires and deprived them of targets. For the rest of the night, Foster walked up and down his line, keeping the men awake, standing with gun in hand, ready to respond to any threat.[244]

Individuals made their way to safety as best they could. The return to friendly lines was a lonely and frustrating one for George Lewis, who wandered the dark woods alone after separating from his comrades at the start of the Confederate charge. He did not know whether he was heading into the arms of his friends or his enemies. One awkward step too many followed by a splash, and he suddenly found himself up to his neck in the Pickett's millpond. But being a Baptist, this did not alarm him to any great extent. Pulling himself out of the pond, he continued searching. The moon rose at approximately 1:00 a.m. and probably helped him and others feel their way through the night. Eventually, at 3:00 a.m. by his estimate, he came upon a group of men huddled in the darkness. Lewis asked who they were, and the reply revealed that it was General Howard and his staff. He gave his name, rank and unit and asked for directions, but none of those present could give any. Feeling it was his duty, he addressed Howard directly. After begging his pardon for the intrusion, Lewis informed him that "there was not so much as a union picket between our lines and the Rebels." This was, of course, false. King's brigade was entrenched, or busy building entrenchments, at the northern end of the Pickett wheat field, and the remnants of Wood's division were doing the same to their right. "There is not a word of truth to your story sir," retorted Howard. "Go away from here. This is my headquarters." Lewis left immediately but wondered to himself how a man who was such a devout Christian and corps commander could "still be so little of a gentleman." This late-night encounter likely did much to influence his harsh opinion of Howard. To be fair to Lewis, the Union line terminated at the creek, and it would have been entirely possible for an individual like him, in the dead of night, to wander around the east side of the creek and make his way back behind the Union lines without encountering any formed resistance. But in Howard's defense, the last thing he needed, stressed, exhausted and sitting in the dark with a bruised foot, was for a lowly captain to tell him his lines were faulty when, in fact, they were indeed perfectly intact. Except for cavalry, the Confederates didn't have anybody on the east side of the creek either.[245]

For his part after his injury, Howard had spent the evening sitting among the wounded. Having established his headquarters behind the lines, staff officers went back and forth coordinating his units, overseeing the construction of breastworks, preparing to repulse a possible Confederate counterattack and working to establish contact with the rest of the army. Howard remained stationary, nursing his wound and working throughout the night. It was a nightmarish scene among the wounded. As he later wrote:

> *That opening in the forest, faint fires here and there revealing men wounded, armless, legless, or eyeless…some with heads bound up with cotton strips, some standing and walking nervously around, some sitting with bended forms, and some prone upon the earth—who can picture it? A few men, in despair, had resorted to drink for relief. The sad sounds from those in pain were mingled with the oaths of the drunken and the more heartless.*[246]

Union soldiers weren't the only ones having trouble finding their own lines. Thomas Stokes of the 10th Texas injured himself during the nighttime charge, falling off one of the many rock outcroppings that littered the slope. While trying to make his way back to the main line he became lost. He later wrote:

> *Here I was, alone in the darkness of midnight with the wounded, the dying, the dead. What an hour of horror! I hope never again to experience such. I am not superstitious, but the great excitement of seven hours of fierce conflict, ending with a bold and I might say reckless charge—for we knew not what was in our front—and then left entirely alone, causes a mental and physical depression that for one to fully appreciate he must be surrounded by the same circumstances. My feelings in battle were nothing to compare to this hour.*

After heading in many different directions, Stokes heard movement in the brush nearby. He commanded the individual to halt and asked what regiment he belonged to. The man replied that he was with the 15th Wisconsin, and Stokes promptly took him prisoner. Forcing the man to walk in front of him, the two continued groping through the woods. Eventually, the duo came upon more men talking in the darkness. When asked the same question, this time the answer was, "Mississippians," which could only be fellow confederates belonging to Walthall's command. Relieved, Stokes entered his own lines, just as the moon was beginning to rise. He could have taken the opportunity to relax but instead felt compelled to venture outside the lines again to see if he could help any of the wounded. He first came upon a Yank shot through the leg who he told they would take care of. Next, he found another shot through the head, wailing "Oh my God! Oh my God!" Stokes tried to comfort the man and asked if there was anything he could do for him. The wounded soldier replied that it would do no good. Stokes assured him that God would have mercy upon him, but the wounded man had drifted away in his delirium.[247]

The Confederates in the cornfield likewise did their best to reorganize after the charge. Amable P. Richards later wrote how his company found each other after the charge. In hoarse whispers, the 4th Louisiana men went along the lines and inquired about their friends. "Have you seen Tom, Martin, George or John…or do you know of any who are hurt?" After they had assembled, Tom Zachary asked them to pray, and the soldiers knelt, offering prayer and praise and thanksgiving for their deliverance.[248]

Both sides did the best they could during the night to improve their positions. The Confederates entrenched where they fought, Granbury's men along the ridge overlooking the ravine. William Smith spent the night as he had the afternoon, going back and forth from his wagon to the men at the works issuing ammunition. During a rest period, he and his party debated amongst themselves whether the moon and the stars were inhabited, a discussion that surely would have made Carl Sagan proud a century later.[249]

Lowrey's men and the 4th Louisiana spent the night where their charge ended along the fence bordering the northern end of the cornfield. They would fall back and begin building breastworks along the spur at the southern end the next day. Farther to the north, Wood's division fell into line to the right of King's brigade. Hazen connected with King, while Gibson's men formed the center and Knepler's brigade fell in on the right. The men began making earthworks immediately, despite being exhausted after fighting all evening. Everyone feared a larger, coordinated Confederate counterattack, and the only way to successfully fight off such an attack was the proven worth of several feet of earth and logs. Howard asked General McLean to extend his brigade even farther to the right in an attempt to link up with the rest of the Twenty-Third Corps, but instead McLean marched his brigade back to his previous day's bivouac. It would be the next afternoon before the two divisions reestablished contact with the Twenty-Third Corps.[250]

Those that had the opportunity slept as best they could. Little did they realize the horrors that would reveal themselves when sunlight once again fell upon the battlefield.

Chapter 16

A Great Blue Carpet

As soon as it got light enough to see on Saturday morning, Captain Foster realized that they had been standing among enemy dead all night long. But such thoughts were fleeting to the captain; dead Yanks were not a new sight to him and took a back seat to the twin desires of hunger and necessity. A little in front of the lines he found discarded Union knapsacks and haversacks. Inside were blankets, oil cloths, tobacco, sewing kits and, more importantly, bacon, crackers and coffee!

As the sun rose above the horizon and chased away the morning twilight, a new company of skirmishers arrived and relieved Foster and his men. Only as they made their way back to their lines, up the slope in the footsteps of their opponents, did the true horror of the battlefield reveal itself. Foster's thoughts on this discovery are worth noting in full:

> *Here I beheld that which I cannot describe and which I hope never see again, dead men meet the eye in every direction, and in one place I stopped and counted 50 dead men in a circle of 30 ft. of me. Men lying in all sorts of shapes… just as they had fallen, and it seems like they have nearly all been shot in the head, and a great number of them have their skulls bursted open and their brains running out, quite a number that way. I have seen many dead men, and seen them wounded and crippled in various ways, have seen their limbs cut off, but I never saw anything before that made me sick like looking at the brains of these men. I do believe that if a soldier could be made to faint, that I would have fainted if I had not passed on and got out of that place as soon as I did.*

The cliché of being able to walk a certain distance on the bodies of dead men was common during the war. However, there is always a kernel of truth to such stories, and none more so than the aftermath of the fight along the ravine at Pickett's Mill. At least half a dozen extant diaries and letters written immediately after the battle mention the number of dead in such a small space. There is no telling how many more accounts did not survive or become published. William Oliphant, whose aunt supplied the flag for the Union regiment that charged his line, wrote, "The field looked as though a great blue carpet had been spread out over the ground. Dead men were every where; they lay in solid lines just as they fell and in many places were in heaps." Thomas Bigbie wrote to his wife, "I never have seen the like of yankeys that was kild in one place. I could of walked 2 or 3 hunderd yards on the bodys of the ded yanks this I seen with my one eyes."[251]

The brutality of the panorama stayed with many long after the war. R.M. Collins, moved by the contrast between the beauty of the rural landscape and the banality of the fruits of war, wrote in his memoir decades later:

> All along in front of the center and left of our brigade the ground was literally covered with dead men. To look upon this and then the beautiful wildwoods, the pretty flowers as they drank in the morning dew, and listen to the sweet notes of the songsters in God's first temples, we were constrained to say, "What is man and his destiny? What a strange thing is the problem of life."

B.L. Ridley, a member of General Stewart's staff, was touched by a scene he came upon while visiting the battlefield the next day. He wrote:

> I have often thought of two little boys that we saw among the dead Federals. They appeared to be about fourteen years old and were exactly alike. Their hands were clasped in death, with "feet to the guns and face to the sky." Although they were enemies, my heart melted at the idea that the little boys must have been twin brothers, and in death's embrace, their spirits had taken flight away from mother and home in the forefront of battle.[252]

Notwithstanding the damage done by solid cannon balls ripping through the ravine, the rapid discharge of so many rifles in such a confined space devastated the intervening flora. The torrent of minié balls passing back and forth between the two opponents shredded saplings two to five inches in diameter that had the misfortune of growing in the dead-line. The smaller underbrush between the two lines was literally swept away.[253]

The reality of life in the field for the often-undersupplied Confederates tugged harder on the stomach than the conscience, and soon the corpses were stripped of anything useful. One private in the 4th Louisiana found a letter on the body of an Ohio soldier and handed it to his lieutenant.

> *Dearest Darling, Alice, 27th May, 1864: I take this time to write on a rest. We are marching hard to flank the Rebels from Atlanta. I know not where we are in this harsh country. The inhabitants are very poor and ignorant creatures. We expect a fight soon. I suspect we will teach the secesh a lesson. If my life should end, my only wish is that I not be buried in this traitorous land.*

The Confederates collected over a thousand rifles from the battlefield. Wood's division supplied enough rifles to the Confederacy that Granbury's entire brigade was able to exchange their Austrian and Belgian rifles for Enfields on the spot.[254]

The scene of the previous day's fight drew the attention of several general officers. Generals Johnston, Hardee, Hood and Polk, as well as numerous brigadier generals, all came and toured the battlefield. They praised the men and the hard fight they had endured, remarking that they had never witnessed so many men piled thicker on all the battlefields they had seen. As they rode over the battlefield, Johnston said to Granbury, "This shall no longer be called Granbury's but shall be known as Johnston's Brigade," an allusion to the fact that having the brigade named after the army commander would be considered a high honor. General Hood, in his frank manner, quietly remarked, "Texans did this, and Texans can do it again."[255]

The presence of so many corpses would soon affect both the health and morale of the men. Especially since, in Granbury's case, they lay so thickly just outside the lines. Officers assigned details of men the task of collecting and burying the dead. Several reported burying between 400 and 500 dead. The Union dead were collected and buried in at least two large pits, and many more were certainly buried individually or in smaller groups. They buried anywhere from 40 to 150 in the larger pits.[256]

The dawn also brought renewed activity along the Union lines. Captain Lewis and the 124th Ohio awoke to discover that their earthworks built during the night faced the wrong way! They spent the morning hurriedly shoveling dirt from one side to the other, reversing the trench. Lieutenant Cope, who had spent the night distributing ammunition to the 15th Ohio, fell asleep from exhaustion next to the prostrate form of Colonel Wallace only to be awoken by shells exploding over his head. The cause of the shelling could very well have been the smoke from numerous campfires once again springing up behind the lines. A Union soldier will not be denied his hot coffee. Unfortunately, this shelling caused a number of casualties, among them General Richard Johnson. He and General King had spent the night together, sharing a large rock for a pillow. At sun up, his cook built a fire in the bottom of a dry creek bed, a secure enough position, but soon numerous other soldiers had fires going. Confederate batteries began firing shells toward the smoke. One shell severed the arm of the 21st Ohio's Colonel Niebling, while another fragment struck Johnson just over the liver. Niebling's field service was over, but Johnson returned to duty two months later.[257]

Lieutenant Woodcock's experience typified those of the Union wounded. His leg wound from the previous evening had stiffened considerably, and he went to have it examined. A surgeon recommended that he visit the field hospital about four miles away. During the evening, pioneers had cut a road connecting isolated divisions to the rest of the army, and ambulances were traveling between the field hospital located behind Johnson's division and the main hospital behind the Fourth Corps lines. Unfortunately for Woodcock, the last batch of ambulances had just left. Still, he wanted to put as much distance as he could between himself and the fighting, so in the company of another walking wounded soldier from the 79th Indiana, he set off on foot. Luckily, an ambulance did happen by, and the two rode the rest of the way. Still, it was a miserable experience. The wagon ambulances of the day lacked any meaningful shock absorbers, and the jostling and bouncing on rough roads was torture to the more grievously wounded lying in stretchers. Those that could sit were lucky; they could balance and brace themselves against the rough ride, or at least attempt to.

The main hospital itself was as good as conditions permitted and, in fact, was quite nice by the day's standards thanks to the resources of the Union home front and industrial base. It was located in a beautiful grove of trees, which provided much needed shade. Large arbors were built to accommodate as many of the wounded as possible. Even so, the battle and the constant skirmishing along the rest of the line soon overwhelmed the space and filled it beyond capacity. When Woodcock dismounted from the ambulance, the sight made him sick. Legs, arms, fingers and toes littered the yard around him. Three tables had been dedicated to amputations and had been continuously in use since midnight. Those in the last agonies of death were left alone and unattended. The medical staff could do nothing for them, and they were so few that their attention had to be concentrated on those they *could* save. Stewards dressed the wounds of those that did not require amputation. The dead were collected together, and the gravediggers did not suffer from lack of work. Woodcock found a small contingent from his regiment and settled in. His wound was dressed, and on May 30, he started northward, eventually arriving in Nashville and getting a furlough to go home and recuperate. He rejoined the 9th Kentucky in their works outside of Atlanta in July.[258]

The casualties were certainly severe, but they failed to knock out Wood's division as a fighting force. Nonetheless, many of the veterans remembered the fight as the severest one they fought during the war, which is saying a lot, since many had lived through Shiloh, Stone's River and Chickamauga. As a whole, Wood reported that his division suffered 210 killed, 921 wounded and 318 missing for a total of 1,449 casualties. At the time, Wood acknowledged that while some of the missing might return, the majority were either killed or wounded and captured by the Confederates. Cleburne reported capturing 232 prisoners, 72 of whom were wounded and sent to his field hospital. Wheeler took in 32. That leaves approximately 264 killed on the field, not counting those wounded who later died from their injuries. The Confederate estimates of the dead they buried, while exaggerated, were not too far off.[259]

Hazen's Second Brigade took a beating, losing 467 men. While the exact strength of the brigade going into battle is unknown, a casualty rate of 20–22 percent is not unreasonable. The 41st Ohio took the highest proportion of casualties at 35 percent, losing 102 of the 271 officers and men that marched into battle. Gibson's men suffered greater than Hazen; 681 men were lost, a little over 200 more. Of the casualty rates that survive, the 49th Ohio lost the most on either side both in terms of total casualties and percentage. Of the 414 men who assaulted the Confederates' position, 203 became casualties—an overall rate of 49 percent. Many of the individual companies were shattered. Company A of the 89th Illinois went into battle with 45 men. When they called roll that night, there were only 11 present. Relatively speaking, Knefler's Third Brigade fared much better with only 301 casualties. This is understandable considering that the brigade did not attempt to carry the enemy position and had only provided covering fire to those evacuating the wounded.[260]

In Johnson's division, Carlin and King did not report any casualties. Scribner's losses are available only from the reports of individual regiments, and those are fragmentary. He probably lost about 123 men. The 37th Indiana and 78th Pennsylvania, who had done the most fighting, took the most casualties, with the 37th losing 57 men and the 78th losing 49.

There are no casualty figures for McLean's brigade, but they were probably minimal. Most, if any, casualties would have occurred on the skirmish line that stretched between his position and the rest of the Twenty-Third Corps. At best estimate, Union casualties at Pickett's Mill were about 230 killed, 1,016 wounded and 319 missing for a total of 1,580.[261]

Confederate casualties were considerably lighter. Cleburne lost 85 killed and 363 wounded for a total of 448. With 4,683 enlisted men on the firing line and probably around 5,035 including officers and file closers, this leaves a casualty rate of 9 percent. The only unit of Quarles's Brigade actively engaged was the 4th Louisiana, and it took 20 casualties. Walthall's Mississippians likely suffered none. Wheeler reported 232 casualties between May 6 and May 30. While there is no way to separate those incurred on May 27, many if not the majority probably happened during the fight on the Pickett farm. A figure of 648 Confederate casualties is a good guess, and not unrealistic.[262]

Union leadership at the brigade level was mediocre but competent. Hazen lost control of his brigade in the dense underbrush of the ravine. Under normal circumstances, this could have been disastrous, but it ultimately led to the Union's best chance for victory. Only the lack of support and the timely arrival of Lowrey's Brigade dashed the hope for a turned flank and a quick victory. Years after the war, Hazen's conduct during the battle was brought on trial—literally. During the court martial of a fellow officer in 1879, the only way that officer could prove his innocence was to disparage Hazen's courage in several battles during the war. However, Captain Briant of the 6th Indiana firmly placed Hazen at the cornfield during the battle, as did Hazen on his own map of the engagement, drawn long before postwar politics and animosities entered the scene. He may not have led from the front, galloping wildly among his men brandishing his sword, but he was no coward, and the court martial agreed. Of the three brigade commanders in Wood's division, Gibson kept his under the best control. The two lines of his brigade drifted, but not by much, and their assault remained narrowly focused on Granbury's Texans. Likewise, Knefler did the best he could given the circumstances. Two of his regiments had drifted into the ravine, but most of his brigade remained under his direct control at the cornfield.[263]

Colonel Scribner's failure to aggressively push forward and support Wood's division—and Hazen's brigade in particular—denied the Union any chance of victory. Letting a line of cavalry skirmishers delay the advance of an entire brigade of veteran infantry was inexcusable. The outcome of a battle between Scribner, Hazen, Lowrey and Quarles in the cornfield will never be known, but Scribner's failure to arrive there certainly doomed any chance Hazen had of turning the Confederate flank. His division commander, Johnson, shares some of the blame for delaying his advance, but the conduct of the timid assault lies squarely on Scribner's shoulders.

At least Scribner tried to get his men into the battle; General McLean didn't even do that. He completely ignored his mission to distract Govan's attention in the large wheat field. This failure gave Cleburne the confidence he needed to release his reserves and send them to the cornfield. McLean never even made his men visible to the enemy. In addition, when Howard ordered him to extend the line during the night and help consolidate the position, he instead marched his men away from the battlefield and back to his starting point. General Sherman may not have mentioned the battle in his official report or his memoir, but even he could not ignore such a blatant failure in a general officer. He had removed a general for botching an attack at Resaca two weeks earlier, and he did so again with McLean. On June 17, Sherman transferred him to the District of Kentucky.[264]

Thomas Wood, for his part, must be faulted for feeding the brigades of his division into the attack one at a time, ensuring defeat. Part of this can be mitigated by Howard's presence. Both attempted to avoid the responsibility for the nature of the attack in postwar writings, but in all likelihood, the two of them conferred on the deployment of the division. The fact that Wood never protested the way his division attacked lends credence to this conclusion. What Wood cannot be faulted for, however, was assaulting an entrenched position. He was specifically ordered not to do so, and he obeyed. When Hazen's brigade crested the ravine, they encountered Granbury's men on the hillside, just deployed and without time to build breastworks. Only during lulls in the fighting did the Confederates manage to throw up crude works of scattered logs and branches.

Ultimately, the defeat at Pickett's Mill belongs to Howard. First, upon arrival at the end of the Confederate line, he delayed his attack by an hour, perhaps as much as two by some estimates. Most importantly, he agreed, or acquiesced, to a piecemeal attack by one division and the commitment of only one brigade out of three from the other. Once the attack started, he failed to personally ensure that his orders were carried out. The distances between the troops under his command were small, and he could have easily ridden over to Johnson to get Scribner's brigade moving in tandem with Hazen. Similarly, he could have personally confronted McLean on his failure to make a show of force in the large wheat field. But he failed to do either, and once wounded during Gibson's assault, he remained in one place nursing his foot and coordinating the battle from there. While it's important to view Howard's decisions in light of what he knew at the time and not with hindsight, it must be remembered that he had positive orders from Sherman to attack the Confederate flank and rear. These orders were reiterated by Thomas in the message received just before the attack. The lack of aggressive leadership, a piecemeal assault and the ultimate failure of the attack all rest squarely on the shoulders of Oliver O. Howard. Still, his failure during the battle did little to hurt his career. It was just one unfortunate setback in the larger campaign. Howard would go on to take command of the Army of the Tennessee in July after McPherson's untimely death outside of Atlanta.

In stark contrast, the Confederate leadership had done almost everything right. General Cleburne conducted a superb defensive battle, beginning the day with three of his four brigades in reserve, ready to respond to any contingency. He sent Govan's entire brigade forward early in the morning to develop the enemy's position and keep him informed of any changes. He had the foresight to clear trails through the forest behind the lines to facilitate the movement of his reserves. Once the battle started, he used those reserves wisely. Recognizing the lack of enemy activity in front of Govan, he pulled a regiment from that unit and sent it to the cornfield just in time, followed closely by Lowrey's entire brigade. He placed Quarles's Brigade in line where it was needed most, and wisely approved a rare night counterattack to clear the Federals from his front. Walthall's arrival likely gave him the peace of mind to approve it. All told, Cleburne's exemplary leadership tipped the balance in the Confederates' favor.

Cleburne's brigadiers gave excellent performances. Polk and Govan didn't have much to do on their front except skirmish, but they kept up a lively front. Govan's men, along with Hotchkiss's artillery, made the large wheat field a dangerous place to be. Granbury did an excellent job getting his men into position along the ridge just before Hazen's arrival and kept his men in place and fighting during extremely close combat. He wisely pushed for and received permission to throw the Federals back after nightfall, ultimately winning the accolades of Joseph Johnston and the rest of the Confederate army. Lowrey handled his brigade expertly, deploying his regiments from column to line one after the other as they cleared the units in front. His aggressive personal leadership won Cleburne's praise.

The other Confederate commanders present acquitted themselves well. General Quarles, like Lowrey, was with his men on the frontline and personally led the 4th Louisiana in its counterattack across the cornfield. John Kelly held his cavalrymen on the ridge overlooking the ravine far longer than they should have, putting up a brave fight and discouraging Scribner from attacking more aggressively. He even charged alongside the 8th & 19th Arkansas in its attempt to shore up Granbury's flank. Even General Wheeler was on hand, coordinating the movements of his two cavalry divisions. Such personal leadership inspires men and makes all the difference between winning and losing.

By the afternoon of May 28, the focus of the fighting along the New Hope line shifted westward toward Dallas. There the Confederates attempted to launch an attack against McPherson, who was isolated from Sherman and the other two Union armies. It was almost a mirror image of the Pickett's Mill fight. But unlike Cleburne, the Union lines were intact and fully entrenched. Realizing this, the Confederate commander canceled the assault, but a misinterpretation of cannon fire for the signal to advance led to a desperate, bloody and unsuccessful charge. During the next week, Sherman switched from trying to flank the Confederates near Dallas to shifting his lines back to Acworth and the railroad. With all of Johnston's infantry along the New Hope line, Sherman's cavalry easily captured Allatoona Pass on June 1. By June 4, Johnston realized his position was hopeless and evacuated the lines in Paulding County that night. For the next month, he would hold Sherman at bay in Cobb County and along the slopes of Kennesaw Mountain.

The Battle of Pickett's Mill was an important engagement along the New Hope line in May 1864. It established the eastern extremity of both lines for several days, and Howard's defeat shifted Sherman's focus toward Dallas and McPherson's safety. It was also one of the most fiercely contested battles fought in such a short span of time and along such a narrow front. Until recently, it was scarcely remembered by any except those who had fought there. As Ambrose Bierce puts it, the battle was truly "foredoomed to oblivion." And yet, it was the soldiers themselves who decided the battle. The struggle along the ravines and fields of the Pickett settlement showcased the bravery and determination of both Union and Confederates struggling for what they believed in with every fiber of their being. It was also a classic example of how leadership can mean the difference between victory and defeat. In the minds and attitudes of its surviving veterans, Pickett's Mill would forever be a "criminal blunder."

Chapter 17

The Park Today

The battlefield today is one of the most if not the most well-preserved battlefields of the Civil War. Opened as a park in 1992, it also has a very interesting history—a tale of relic hunters, amateur historians, large corporations and the Georgia legislature. Few parks have such a varied and storied tale to tell and still come out as they looked over a century and a half ago.

For several decades, the land remained in private hands, with many small farms dotting the area around the battlefield. Land was cultivated, earthworks were leveled and life moved on. This changed, however, beginning in August 1932, when C.E. McMichen bought several land lots of the battlefield. In 1951, he and his brother purchased an additional 300 acres. In 1952, the McMichen brothers sold 200 of these acres to the North Georgia Timberland Company to accompany an additional 54 acres that same year. All told, this left the timber company in the possession of 395 acres of core battlefield property.

The timber company wasn't the only one interested in the land. During the 1930s, famed Civil War relic hunter Beverly Dubose and noted Atlanta historian Wilbur Kurtz mapped the area along the New Hope line. They were well aware of the existence of the battlefield but chose to keep it a secret, most likely to protect Dubose's relic-hunting interests. They left a discrete metal marker on a concrete base at the intersection of Mount Tabor Church Road and the old overgrown Pickett's Mill Road to mark the entrance to the property. In the 1950s, historian Philip Secrist, working only from the descriptions left in the Official Records, rediscovered the battlefield. After several years studying the battle and the land, he published his discovery in the May 1971 issue of Civil War Times Illustrated.

Events began to unfold rapidly. Upon learning that Georgia Kraft (formerly the North Georgia Timber Company) was interested in selling portions of the land, Secrist and four other investors formed a corporation and bought the land, eventually purchasing 467.76 acres from the company. The Georgia state government also began to express interest in the site. Governor Jimmy Carter established a commission to study and report on preserving sites throughout the state, and Pickett's Mill was to be the case study. Plans were made to make a series of parks along the Dallas/New Hope/Pickett's Mill line, but only Pickett's Mill was chosen for development because of its pristine condition. The state purchased the 467.76 acres from Secrist and his investors in July 1973. Even newly elected Georgia state speaker of the house Tom Murphy expressed interest in the park, demanding to know when it would be completed and what progress had been made.[265]

Roy Dickens and Richard Williams of the Georgia Department of Natural Resources, with the cooperation of the Anthropology Department of Georgia State University, conducted surveys of the land in the years after its purchase, beginning in late 1973. In conjunction with Sydney Kerkis, another local historian who had first visited the property in the late 1940s and spoken with many elderly locals about the battlefield, the three carried out an informal survey of the area. They marked the main surviving features, which included existing trenches, house foundations, roadbeds, gravesites and a Federal field hospital. They also collected various artifacts and did much to identify many of the scenes of heavy fighting.

One feature they did not locate were the mass graves described in many of the Confederate letters and autobiographies. Even a Federal officer, tasked with disinterring the remains of dead Union soldiers on the battlefield, could not find any mass graves when he visited the site in 1866, a mere two years after the battle. Such large pits would still have been visible after such short a time. And General Wood himself, visiting the site just after the Confederates evacuated it, mentioned in his report "several lines of trenches (capable of containing from twenty-five to forty bodies) on the battlefield outside of the enemy's intrenchments [sic]." What happened to these burial pits remains a mystery.[266]

The surveys continued in 1977–78 with the excavation of the Brandt house on the eastern side of the creek. By 1981, the park had expanded to 700 acres, encompassing the entirety of the battlefield and much of the surrounding approaches and environs. The park was dedicated on May 24, 1990, and opened to the public in May 1992.

Today, the battlefield exists much as it did that hot day in May 1864. Most of the 1864 roads are still there, and the rural nature of Paulding County at the time of the purchase ensured that no main highways or developments had encroached upon the land. The three main fields—the large and small wheat fields and the cornfield—survive and have been restored, although they are not as large as they were at the time of the battle. The location of endangered species of flora has prevented the park from expanding the fields to their battlefield size. There are no monuments dedicated to the regiments and brigades that fought there to clutter the view. The only man-made concessions to the park are the visitors' center (located behind Granbury's line), the road connecting it to the entrance at Mount Tabor Church Road, interpretive trails allowing visitors to access and view the critical areas of the battle and wooden bridges across Pickett's Mill Creek.

Still, the park has not escaped the ravages of time unscathed. Recent events have taken a toll on the park. In 2009, record rains and flooding washed away all the bridges across the creek. In 2010 and 2011, a pine beetle infestation threatened the forest within the park. Scores of acres had to be thinned or removed to preserve the core of the battlefield from being infested and ruined. While such efforts saved that inner core, much of the outlying forest was thinned and cut, in one case all the way to the southern edge of the hard-fought-over cornfield. It will take decades for the trees to grow again and return the view to its natural state.

Pickett's Mill Battlefield Historic Site
4432 Mount Tabor Church Road
Dallas, GA 30157

http://www.gastateparks.org/PickettsMillBattlefield

Appendix

Order of Battle

Trying to piece together the strength of units that fought in a Civil War battle is a puzzle—a puzzle with pieces that are missing, don't match or have multiples that are supposed to fit in the same place. Great battles such as Gettysburg, where the numbers are supposedly set in stone, are still open to interpretation. Even for a small battle such as Pickett's Mill, it's not as easy as simply opening a book and finding the exact numbers. In order to compare "apples to apples," you have to do some digging and use a few mathematical equations and guesswork. Even the most revered studies such as Livermore's *Numbers and Losses in the Civil War* that many take for granted when citing battle strengths are a product of guesswork and mathematics, not hard numbers gleaned from the *Official Records* and other primary sources.

The closest method of reporting soldiers between the two armies was a category called Present for Duty (PFD), which included enlisted men, officers, NCOs and often a few noncombatants, such as musicians, who nonetheless had an important function during combat. The other, less common figure is "effectives." This can be misleading, however, as it had a different meaning for the two armies. For the Confederates, it meant only those actually on the firing line and excluded officers, file closers and non-combatants. For the Federals, however, Sherman issued a directive that all members of a unit were to be included in the "effective" category, essentially making it equivalent to PFD.[267] In all cases in the Order of Battle, the attempt was made to translate the number into PFD, according to the formula used by Livermore and Newton. Original use of PFD or "effective" is clarified in the notes.[268]

	Strength	KIA	WIA	MIA	Total
UNION					
Army of the Cumberland	15,869				
Fourth Army Corps					
Major General Oliver O. Howard					
Third Division[269]	7,092				
Brigadier General Thomas J. Wood					
1st Brigade					
Colonel William H. Gibson					
35th Illinois					
89th Illinois[270]		16	71	67	154
32nd Indiana					
15th Ohio[271]		19	64	19	102
49th Ohio[272]	414	52	147	4	203
15th Wisconsin					
2nd Brigade					
Brigadier General William B. Hazen					
6th Indiana[273]	474	15	15	11	41
5th Kentucky					
6th Kentucky					
23rd Kentucky					
1st Ohio					
41st Ohio[274]	271	26	70	6	102
93rd Ohio[275]		11	32	6	49
124th Ohio[276]		18	44	10	72

	Strength	KIA	WIA	MIA	Total
UNION					
3rd Brigade					
Colonel Frederick Knefler					
79th Indiana[277]		3	16		19
9th Kentucky[278]		4	16		20
17th Kentucky[279]		1	43		44
13th Ohio[280]	200	6	27	26	59
19th Ohio[281]					45
59th Ohio[282]		1	29	16	45
86th Indiana[283]			20		20

Fourteenth Army Corps
First Division   7,277
Brigadier General Richard W. Johnson

1st Brigade
Brigadier General William P. Carlin
104th Illinois
42nd Indiana
88th Indiana
15th Kentucky
2nd Ohio
33rd Ohio
94th Ohio
10th Wisconsin
21st Wisconsin

2nd Brigade
Brigadier General John H. King

	Strength	KIA	WIA	MIA	Total
UNION					
11th Michigan					
69th Ohio					
1st & 3rd Bns 15th U.S.					
2nd Bn 15th U.S.					
1st Bn. 16th U.S.					
2nd Bn. 16th U.S.					
1st & 3rd Bns 18th U.S.					
2nd Bn. 18th U.S.					
1st & 2nd Bns. 19th U.S.					
3rd Brigade					
Colonel Benjamin F. Scribner					
37th Indiana[284]		13	43	1	57
38th Indiana[285]			2		2
21st Ohio[286]	414				
74th Ohio					
78th Pennsylvania[287]		5	44		49
1st Wisconsin					

Twenty-Third Army Corps

Second Division

	Strength
1st Brigade[288]	1,500
Brigadier General Nathaniel C. McLean	
80th Indiana	
13th Kentucky	
25th Michigan[289]	210
3rd Tennessee[290]	255
6th Tennessee	

	Strength	KIA	WIA	MIA	Total

CONFEDERATE

Army of Tennessee   8,789

Hardee's Corps

Cleburne's Division[291]   5,213

Major General Patrick R. Cleburne

Polk's Brigade

Brigadier General Lucius Polk

1st & 15th Arkansas (Consolidated)

5th Confederate

2nd Tennessee

48th Tennessee

Govan's Brigade

Brigadier General Daniel C. Govan

2nd & 24th Arkansas (Consolidated)

5th & 13th Arkansas (Consolidated)

6th & 7th Arkansas (Consolidated)

8th & 19th Arkansas (Consolidated)

3rd Confederate

Lowrey's Brigade

Brigadier General Mark P. Lowrey

16th Alabama

33rd Alabama

45th Alabama

32nd Mississippi

45th Mississippi

	Strength	KIA	WIA	MIA	Total

CONFEDERATE

Granbury's Brigade
Brigadier General Hiram B. Granbury
6th Texas Infantry & 15th
Texas Cavalry (Consolidated)
7th Texas
10th Texas
17th & 18th Texas Cavalry (Consolidated)
24th & 25th Texas Cavalry (Consolidated)

Hotchkiss' Battalion[292]   339
Key's Arkansas Battery
Semple's Alabama Battery
Warren's Mississippi Battery

Hindman's Division

Walthall's Brigade[293]   1,086
Brigadier General Edward Walthall
24th & 27th Mississippi (Consolidated)[294]   519
29th & 30th Mississippi (Consolidated)[295]   384
34th Mississippi[296]   183

Army of Mississippi (Polk's Corps)

Quarles's Brigade[297]   1,329
Brigadier General William Quarles
4th Louisiana[298]   360
30th Louisiana[299]   340
42nd Tennessee

	Strength	KIA	WIA	MIA	Total

CONFEDERATE

46th & 55th Tennessee (Consolidated)

48th Tennessee

49th Tennessee

53rd Tennessee

Cavalry Corps[300]   822 (1,405)

Major General Joseph Wheeler

Kelly's Division[301]   822 (1,405)

Brigadier General John Kelly

Hannon's Brigade[302]   620

Colonel Moses Hannon

53rd Alabama

24th Alabama

Allen's Brigade[303]   785

Brigadier General William Allen

3rd Confederate

8th Confederate

10th Confederate

12th Confederate

Notes

Chapter 1

1. U.S. War Department, *The War of the Rebellion: A Compilation of the Official Records of the Union and Confederate Armies.* Series 1, vol. 38, part I, 115. Hereafter, the work will be cited as *Official Records*. All references are to Series 1 unless otherwise indicated.
2. *Official Records*, vol. 38, part III, 676.

Chapter 2

3. Cope, *The Fifteenth Ohio Volunteers*, 446.
4. Bigger, *Ohio's Silver-Tongued Orator*, 276–78.
5. Bigger, *Ohio's Silver-Tongued Orator,* 313–14.
6. Cope, *The Fifteenth Ohio Volunteers,* 241–42, 269–71.
7. Lewis, *Campaigns of the 124th*, 146.
8. Hazen, *A Narrative of Military Service*, 1, 432.
9. *Official Records*, vol. 38, part I, 421.
10. Bierce, *Collected Works,* 284.
11. Noe, *A Southern Boy in Blue*, 288.
12. Beszedits. "Frederick Knefler"; *Official Records*, vol. 38, part I, 454.

13. Beatty, *The Citizen-Soldier*, 235–36.

14. Warner, *Generals in Blue*, 569.

15. Cozzens, *This Terrible Sound*, 363–75.

16. *Official Records*, vol. 30, part IV, 209.

17. *Official Records*, vol. 32, part III, 258.

18. Howard, *Autobiography*, 81–83.

19. Howard, *Autobiography*, 374.

20. Fox, *Regimental Losses*, 87.

21. Howe, *Home Letters of General Sherman*, 303.

22. Castel, *Decision in the West*, 131, 163–65.

23. Howard, *Autobiography*, 537

24. Howard, *Autobiography*, 535–36

25. Sherman, *Memoirs of*, 42.

26. *Official Records*, vol. 38, part IV, 272.

27. *Official Records*, vol. 38, part IV, 288–89.

28. *Official Records*, vol. 38, part I, 560-561; Calkins, *The History of the One Hundred and Fourth Regiment*, 207; *History of the Organization*, 178.

29. Perry, *History of the Thirty-Eighth Regiment*, 134-135; Price, *One Year in the Civil War*, 13.

CHAPTER 3

30. Gay, *Life in Dixie*, 86; Castel, *Decision in the West*, 217.

31. Johnston, *Narrative of Military Operations*, 325.

32. *Official Records*, vol. 38, part III, 724.

33. Smith, *Diary*, May 23.

34. Watkins, *"Co. Aytch,"* 134.

35. Fowler, *Diary*, May 22.

36. Foster, *One of Cleburne's Command*, 79.

37. Ibid., 80.

38. *Official Records*, vol. 38, part III, 643.

39. *Official Records*, vol. 38, part III, 676.

40. Castel, *Decision in the West*, 216; *Official Records*, vol. 38, part III, 616; Johnston, *Narrative*, 325; Wheeler's Confederate Cavalry Association, *Campaigns of Wheeler*, 185.

CHAPTER 4

41. *Official Records*, vol. 38, part IV, 289–91.

42. *Official Records*, vol. 38, part IV, 295; Cope, *The Fifteenth Ohio Volunteers*, 446–47; Noe, *A Southern Boy in Blue*, 289.

43. Briant, *History of the Sixth Regiment*, 314–15; *History of the Seventy-Ninth Regiment Indiana Volunteer Infantry*, 139. Barrett's Mill is also sometimes referred to as Milner's Mill. On the map in the *Official Atlas*, it is labeled as Milner and Barrett's Mill.

44. *Official Records*, vol. 38, part IV, 296.

45. Price, *One Year in the Civil War*, 13; Dyer, *A Compendium of the*, 1644.

46. Reid, *Ohio in the War*, 921–22; Hennessy, *Return to Bull Run*, 383–93.

47. Owens, *Green County Soldiers*, 70; Otto, *Diary*, May 23.

48. Puntenney, *History of the Thirty-Seventh Regiment*, 88; Perry, *History of the Thirty-Eighth*, 135; Owens, *Green County Soldiers*, 70.

49. Owens, *Green County Soldiers*, 70–71.

50. Ottos, *Diary*, May 23.

51. *Official Records*, vol. 38, part I, 593.

52. Scribner, *How Soldiers Were Made*, 12–19, 221; Starkweather, *Statement of Military Services*, 9.

53. Johnson, *Body of Brave Men*, xxxiii, 43–44.

54. *Official Records*, vol. 38, part IV, 17-18.

55. *Official Records*, vol. 38, part IV, 737; Wheeler's Confederate Cavalry Association, *Campaigns of Wheeler*, 185.

56. *Official Records*, vol. 38, part IV, 737-38; Johnston, *Narrative*, 326.

57. Foster, *One of Cleburne's Command*, 80; Fowler, *Diary*, May 23; Smith, *Diary*, May 23.

58. *Official Records*, vol. 38, part IV, 738-39.

CHAPTER 5

59. *Official Records*, vol. 38, part IV, 299-300.

60. *History of the Seventy-Ninth*, 139; Stahl, *Diary*, May 24; Cox, *Military Reminiscences*, 237.

61. *Official Records*, vol. 38, part IV, 300; Barnes, et al., *The Eighty-Sixth Regiment*, 358; *History of the Seventy-Ninth*, 139; *Battery M, First Regiment Illinois Light Artillery*, 181.

62. Cope, *The Fifteenth Ohio Volunteers*, 447; *Battery M, First Regiment Illinois Light Artillery* 181.

63. Cope, *The Fifteenth Ohio Volunteers*, 447; Noe, *A Southern Boy in Blue*, 289; Lewis, *Campaigns of the 124th*, 146.

64. Stahl, *Diary*, May 24; Cope, *The Fifteenth Ohio Volunteers*, 447.

65. *Official Records*, vol. 38, part I, 522–23.

66. Ottos, *Diary*, May 24.

67. *Official Records*, vol. 38, part I, 523.

68. Price, *One Year in the Civil War*, 14; Cox, *Military Reminiscence*, 239.

69. *Official Records*, vol. 38, part III, 947–49; Wheeler's Confederate Cavalry Association, *Campaigns of Wheeler*, 185–87; *Official Records*, vol. 38, part I, 143.

70. Foster, *One of Cleburne's Command*, 80; *Official Records*, vol. 38, part IV, 739; Fowler, *Diary*, May 24.

71. Smith, *Diary*, May 24.

72. *Official Records*, vol. 38, part IV, 742; *Official Records*, vol. 38, part III, 705.

CHAPTER 6

73. *Official Records*, vol. 38, part II, 511; *Official Records*, vol. 38, part IV, 307–08

74. *Official Records*, vol. 38, part IV, 308; *History of the Seventy-Ninth*, 139–40; Cope, *The Fifteenth Ohio Volunteers*, 447.

75. Barnes, et al., *The Eighty-Sixth Regiment*, 359–60.

76. *Official Records*, vol. 38, part II, 122–23; Kerksis, *The Atlanta Papers*, 407. Lieutenant Colonel Henry Stone on Thomas's staff clearly states that Geary took the wrong turn before reaching Pumpkinvine Creek.

77. Johnston, *Narrative*, 326; *Official Records*, vol. 38, part III, 833; *Official Records*, vol. 38, part II, 123.

78. *Official Records*, vol. 38, part II, 123.

79. *Official Records*, vol. 38, part I, 192–93, 862; Cope, *The Fifteenth Ohio Volunteers*, 447; *History of the Seventy-Ninth*, 139–40.

80. *Official Records*, vol. 38, part I, 192–93, 862.

81. Cope, *The Fifteenth Ohio Volunteers*, 447–48.

82. *Official Records*, vol. 38, part I, 192–93, 862.

83. Stahl, *Diary*, May 25; *History of the Seventy-Ninth*, 140; Noe, *A Southern Boy in Blue*, 290; Barnes, et al., *The Eighty-Sixth Regiment*, 360; *Official Records*, vol. 38, part I, 863.

84. Howard, *Autobiography*, 547, 549.

85. *Official Records*, vol. 38, part II, 567, 680; Cox, *Military Reminiscence*, 240–41; Howard, *Autobiography*, 547–48.

86. Smith, *Diary*, May 24; Foster, *One of Cleburne's Command*, 80–81; Hay, *Cleburne and His Command*, 218.

87. Hay, *Cleburne and His Command*, 218; Spurlin, *Diary of Charles A. Leuschner*, 33–34; *Official Records*, vol. 38, part IV, 742–43; Foster, *One of Cleburne's Command*, 81. Although no orders survive in the *Official Records*, firsthand accounts all agree that Cleburne's Division resumed its march toward Dallas at nightfall, several hours before Hardee penned his 10:30 p.m. order to set off for the Mauldin house at 4:00 a.m.

CHAPTER 7

88. *Official Records*, vol. 38, part II, 124.

89. *Official Records*, vol. 38, part I, 193, 333, 354; *Official Records*, vol. 38, part II, 124.

90. Cope, *The Fifteenth Ohio Volunteers*, 449; *Official Records*, vol. 38, part I, 193, 392; Hazen, *Narrative*, 254.

91. Cope, *The Fifteenth Ohio Volunteers*, 449; Hazen, *Narrative*, 254.

92. Cope, *The Fifteenth Ohio Volunteers*, 449; *Official Records*, vol. 38, part II, 680.

93. Cope, *The Fifteenth Ohio Volunteers*, 449-50; Hazen, *Narrative*, 254; *Official Records*, vol. 38, part I, 392, 418, 446. There is some discrepancy as to when the advance across Possum Creek started. Hazen puts the time as early as 7:00 a.m., but surely that is much too early. Colonel Gibson's report states that they advanced at 9:00 a.m., while Alexis Cope in the 15th Ohio's regimental history states that they were served dinner just before attacking. Since it is not unreasonable to think they would serve dinner (lunch) around 9:00 a.m. (they had been up since 3:00 a.m. after all), I went with 9:00 a.m. for the time of the advance.

94. *Official Records*, vol. 38, part I, 392; Brandley, "Lively Times for Co. C."; Cope, *The Fifteenth Ohio Volunteers*, 449–50.

95. Cox, *Military Reminiscence*, 241; *Official Records*, vol. 38, part II, 680.

96. *Official Records*, vol. 38, part II, 567, 599–600, 626; Price, *One Year in the Civil War*, 14–15. The 24th Alabama was part of Manigault's Brigade, Hindman's Division, which moved up beside Stevenson's Division earlier in the morning.

97. *Official Records*, vol. 38, part II, 599, 612, 680.

98. *Official Records*, vol. 38, part I, 506, 523; *Official Records*, vol. 38, part IV, 316–17, 324.

99. Perry, *History of the Thirty-Eighth Regiment*, 136.

100. *Official Records*, vol. 38, part I, 529.

101. *Official Records*, vol. 38, part III, 34, 95.

102. Ibid., 761.

103. *Official Records*, vol. 38, part III, 724; Foster, *One of Cleburne's Command*, 81–82. The identity of the Georgia unit is not stated, but odds are it was Alfred Cumming's brigade of Georgia troops in Stevenson's Division. Cleburne's Division itself had no Georgia regiments, and neither did Hindman's. Cumming's Brigade had the only Georgia troops in Stevenson's Division. Stovall's Brigade in Stewart's Division was composed of Georgia men, but they were back at New Hope Church, and Foster's description makes it sound like they were at or near the end of their march. Walker's Division was composed almost entirely of Georgia units, but being in reserve at New Hope Church, it wasn't on the frontline as described. Alfred Cumming's men seem the most logical choice.

104. Smith, *Diary*, May 26; *Official Records*, vol. 38, part III, 724; Sneed, *Letter to Wife*.

105. Smith, *Diary*, May 26.

CHAPTER 8

106. *History of the Seventy-Ninth*, 140.

107. *Official Records*, vol. 38, part IV, 323.

108. *History of the Seventy-Ninth*, 140; *Official Records*, vol. 38, part I, 386; Lewis, *Campaigns of the 124th*, 147–48; Howard, *Autobiography*, 553–54. It is impossible to know whether Hampson was killed by a sharpshooter aiming specifically at him or a random bullet. The sharpshooter reference used in the text comes from General Wood.

109. *Official Records*, vol. 38, part I, 193–94; Strahl, *Diary*, May 27; Hazen, *Narrative*, 256.

110. *Official Records*, vol. 38, part III, 724.

111. *Official Records*, vol. 38, part II, 623–24.

112. Ibid., 624.

113. *Official Records*, vol. 38, part I, 194.

114. *Official Records*, vol. 38, part II, 612, 624.

115. Ibid., 635–36.

116. Ibid., 612, 624–25, 638–39.

117. Fowler, *Diary*, May 27; Bourne. "Govan's Brigade," 89; *Official Records*, vol. 38, part IV, 744.

118. Willis, *Old Enough to Die*, 118.

119. *Official Records*, vol. 38, part I, 194, 377; Strahl, *Diary*, May 27.

120. *Official Records*, vol. 38, part I, 423; Kimberly and Holloway, *Forty-First Ohio*, 83; Lewis, *Campaigns of the 124th*, 148.

121. *Official Records*, vol. 38, part I, 392.

122. Ibid., 446.

123. Ibid., 523.

124. Kimberly and Holloway, *The Forty-First Ohio*, 83.

125. Perry, *History of the Thirty-Eighth Regiment*, 137.

126. *Official Records*, vol. 38, part III, 724–25; Hay, *Cleburne and His Command*, 219; Purdue and Howell, *Pat Cleburne*, 323; Joslyn, ed., *Meteor Shining Brightly*, 218; Hurley, "Govan's Brigade," 75. There are conflicting reports concerning the exact position of the 6th & 7th Arkansas and its relation to the section of Key's howitzers sent to fire down the ravine. Lieutenant Bostick on Govan's staff, who wrote a very detailed account in several letters in the weeks after the battle, stated that the right of the 6th & 7th ended at the edge of the large wheat field. Unfortunately, his only reference to Key's battery is that it was in the "center right of the brigade," with no mention of the battery being split between two sections. He also mentions that the regiment could fire into the flank of any units in the ravine. This would only be possible if part of the regiment was refused from the main brigade line and extended across the Leverett Mill Road. Stan Hurley later wrote that the regiment had two distinct wings: the right wing at the head of the ravine, which was bearing the brunt of the assault along with Granbury's men, and the left wing positioned to fire into the enemy's flank. He also mentioned artillery stationed just to the left of the regiment and firing with the left wing into the flank of the Federals. This could only have been Key's section. The regiment had to have extended past the road, with the battery positioned at or near the center of the regiment.

127. Collins, *Chapters from the Unwritten History*, 211.

128. Foster, *One of Cleburne's Command*, 82.

129. Smith, *Diary*, May 27.

130. Richey, *Tirailleurs*, 139–40.

131. *Official Records*, vol. 38, part I, 194, 377, 392, 441, 446, 594; *History of the Seventy-Ninth*, 140–414; McDermott, "A Fierce Hour." Almost all accounts agree that the two divisions began their advance around 11:00 a.m.

132. McMahon, "Pickett's Mills."
133. Official Records, vol. 38, part II, 625.
134. Brandley, "Lively Times for Co. C."; McDermott, A Fierce Hour."; Cope, *The Fifteenth Ohio Volunteers*, 450–51.
135. Kimberly, *The Forty-First Ohio*, 84; *Official Records*, vol. 38, part I, 865; *Official Records*, vol. 38, part II, 625, 680. The Fourth Corps journal puts the time when the column first encountered the Rebel line at 1:45 pm.
136. Lewis, *The Campaigns of the 124th*, 148; Scribner, *How Soldiers Were Made*, 238; *Official Records*, vol. 38, part I, 194; *Official Records*, vol. 38, part II, 680; Price, *One Year in the Civil War*, 15.
137. Scribner, *How Soldiers Were Made*, 238–40.
138. Noe, *A Southern Boy in Blue*, 290–91; *History of the Seventy-Ninth*, 141.
139. *Official Records*, vol. 38, part I, 194, 865; Howard, *Autobiography*, 551–52; Wood, "Pickett's Mill"; Johnson, *A Soldier's Reminiscences*, 277–78. Howard, Johnson and Wood each remember the incident a little differently. Howard puts Stinson's wounding an hour before they reached their final assembly. The Fourth Corps journal kept by Assistant Adjutant General Lieutenant Colonel Joseph S. Fullerton generally agrees with Howard, stating that it was between 3:00 and 3:30 before they arrived at the final assembly point. Wood remembers it happening after they had arrived and were forming for the attack. Johnson says nothing about the timing. Since the Fourth Corps journal was recorded on the field of battle in real time, its timeline has been given preference. Neither Howard nor Wood mention Johnson being there. In his report, however, Howard clearly states that Wood was with him when they observed the end of the Confederate line. Howard noted that Stinson stepped out into the opening to try out his new field glass, whereas Wood stated that they remained behind the cover of the foliage and Stinson disturbed the underbrush enough to warrant a Rebel bullet fired in that direction. Both Howard and Wood agree that Stinson was revived by the use of whiskey, and Wood's account is more detailed on that matter. Modern readers should be amused to know that both generals considered the whiskey to be a stimulant, when, in fact, alcohol is a depressant.
140. Cope, *The Fifteenth Ohio Volunteers*, 451; Kimberly, *The Forty-First Ohio*, 84; Howard, *Autobiography*, 552.

Chapter 9

141. *Official Records*, vol. 38, part I, 865; *Official Records*, vol. 38, part IV, 324.
142. *Official Records*, vol. 38, part I, 194, 472, 478–79, 523, 594; Scribner, *How Soldiers Were Made*, 240–41.
143. Foster, *One of Cleburne's Command*, 82; Newton, *Lost for the Cause*, 264, 266; *Official Records*, vol. 32, part III, 866; *Official Records*, vol. 38, part III, 948.
144. Noe, *A Southern Boy in Blue*, 291.
145. *Official Records*, vol. 38, part II, 680-81.
146. Bierce, *Collected Works*, 286; Kiene Jr., *Civil War Diary*, 229; Franklin, "Under a Terrible Fire."
147. Brandley, "Lively Times for Co. C"; Hazen, *Autobiography*, 257; Bierce, *Collected Works*, 286. It is possible that Brandley only heard part of the conversation and recorded only what he heard Howard say to Hazen. Wood telling Howard to "put Hazen in" could have been part of another discussion, but it seems unlikely that all the participants would come together twice to have two separate conversations concerning Hazen's role in the attack. Hazen and Bierce's version of the event corroborate each other on what Wood said to Howard but do not mention Howard stressing the sacrifice of his brigade. However, Bierce does say that Howard assented, so it's still possible that Howard said it as Brandley remembered and Bierce merely forgot or didn't bother to write it down in his essay. Additionally, neither Howard nor Wood took responsibility for or explain why the attack was made piecemeal instead of with the division column.
148. *Official Records*, vol. 38, part I, 194.
149. *Official Records*, vol. 38, part I, 865; Howard, *Autobiography*, 553. Hazen and Wood put the time of the attack at 4:30 p.m. The Fourth Corps journal says 4:55. In his autobiography, Howard states that it was 5:30, which is clearly too late. Some regimental commanders, such as those of the 41st and 124th Ohio, say 4:00 p.m. One must remember that watches were not synchronized, so the memory of individual officers may well be correct. The time given in the Fourth Corps journal was used in the text, since subsequent events showed that each brigade attacked roughly an hour apart. This includes the time needed to march from the assembly point to contact with the enemy.
150. Brandley, "Lively Times for Co. C."

Chapter 10

151. *Official Records*, vol. 38, part III, 724; Collins, *Unwritten History*, 211–12.

152. Collins, *Unwritten History*, 212; Sneed, Letter to Wife; Bourne, *Confederate Veteran*, 89.

153. Hamilton, "Battle of New Hope Church," 338.

154. Bierce, *Collected Works*, 287–88; Briant, *History of the Sixth*, 316–17.

155. Foster, *One of Cleburne's Command*, 83; Sneed, Letter to Wife; Yeary, ed., *Reminiscences of the Boys in Gray*, 670.

156. McMahon, "Pickett's Mills"; *Official Records*, vol. 38, part I, 435, 442; Kimberly, *The Forty-First Ohio*, 84; Lewis, *The Campaigns of the 124th*, 148–49.

157. Spurlin, *Diary of Charles A. Leuschner*, 34; Bierce, *Collected Works*, 289.

158. *Official Records*, vol. 38, part III, 725; Bierce, *Collected Works*, 291–92.

159. Sneed, Letter to Wife.

160. Kimberly, *The Forty-First Ohio*, 85.

161. Gay, *Life in Dixie*, 88.

162. Lewis, *The Campaigns of the 124th*, 149–51.

163. *Official Records*, vol. 38, part I, 435; Willis, *Old Enough*, 119–20; Kimberly, *The Forty-First Ohio*, 85.

164. *Official Records*, vol. 38, part I, 194-95, 378; Sutherland, ed., *Reminiscences of a Private*, 169–71.

165. Smith, *Diary*, May 27.

166. *Official Records*, vol. 38, part I, 435, 442; *Official Records*, vol. 38, part III, 725.

167. *Official Records*, vol. 38, part III, 725; Collins, *Unwritten History*, 212; Willis, *Old Enough*, 121; Brock, ed., *Southern Historical Society Papers*, 371–72.

168. Briant, *History of the Sixth*, 317–18; Brandley, "Lively Times for Co. C"; Johnston, *Four Months in Libby*, 161–62. There is some confusion regarding the actual location of the 6th Kentucky during the battle. Hazen places the regiment near the center of the line, to the right of the 5th Kentucky, as does the literature at the Pickett's Mill Historic Site. However, no explanation is given as to why the regiment split with the other unit in the battalion, the 23rd Kentucky. The 23rd Kentucky was clearly on the far left near the branch on the east side of the cornfield, as corroborated by both Arnold Brandley of the 23rd and Charles Briant of the 6th Indiana. Captain Isaac Johnston, the commander of the 6th Kentucky during the Atlanta Campaign, places the regiment behind the 23rd in the cornfield, with its flank refused. Brandley mentions troops

behind them, but that they were too far back to do any good. He could have been referring to Scribner's men, but they would have been on the other side of the ridge and at least four hundred yards away. More than likely he was talking about the 6th Kentucky in the cornfield behind him. Gregory McDermott of the 23rd Kentucky mentions a soldier from the 6th Kentucky getting shot behind him and that the two regiments were consolidated during the battle. Taking all the evidence into account, it seems most likely that the 6th and 23rd Kentucky stayed together as a battalion and that the 6th fought in the cornfield behind the 23rd, facing east. If the 6th Kentucky originally formed in the first line as Hazen reported, they quickly sorted themselves out and formed on the left of the 23rd Kentucky. They certainly didn't remain on the left of the 124th Ohio during the battle, and there is no evidence that they remained on the right of the 5th Kentucky and engaged the counterattacking 8th & 19th Arkansas and 33rd Alabama.

169. Brandley, "Lively Times for Co. C."

170. Briant, *History of the Sixth*, 318.

171. *Official Records*, vol. 38, part III, 725; Brock, *Southern Historical Society Papers*, 371–72.

172. Briant, *History of the Sixth*, 318-19.

173. Brandley, "Lively Times for Co. C."

174. *Official Records*, vol. 38, part III, 725; Hay, *Cleburne and His Command*, 219–20; Collins, *Unwritten History*, 212–13; Brock, *Southern Historical Society Papers*, 371–72.

175. Sneed, Letter to Wife.

176. Briant, *History of the Sixth*, 319; Brandley, "Lively Times for Co. C."

177. Briant, *History of the Sixth*, 319–20; Brandley, "Lively Times for Co. C."

178. Brandley, "Lively Times for Co. C."

179. Hazen, *Narrative*, 258; McDermott, "A Fierce Hour."

180. *Official Records*, vol. 38, part III, 725.

CHAPTER 11

181. *Official Records*, vol. 38, part I, 594; Scribner, *How Soldiers Were Made*, 241.

182. Gibson, ed., *History of the Seventy-Eighth*, 147.

183. *Official Records*, vol. 38, part I, 594–95, 605, 865.

184. *Official Records*, vol. 38, part I, 595, 605; Puntenney, *History of the Thirty-Seventh*, 89; Gibson, *History of the Seventy-Eighth*, 148; Duff, Letter to his Aunt Teresa. The fight along the ridge above the Pickett homestead must have been a short one. None of the participants from Scribner's brigade mention much of a fight until the 78th Pennsylvania and 37th Indiana stopped along the summit overlooking Wildcat Branch. They apparently spent the entire battle in this location.

185. Puntenney, *History of the Thirty-Seventh*, 91.

186. *Official Records*, vol. 38, part I, 605; *Official Records*, vol. 38, part III, 940; Puntenney, *History of the Thirty-Seventh*, 90; Gibson, *History of the Seventy-Eighth*, 148.

187. *Official Records*, vol. 38, part I, 595, 608, 613; Perry, *History of the Thirty-Eighth*, 137; Hoskins, "Scribner's Brigade."

188. *Official Records*, vol. 38, part I, 435, 442.

189. *Official Records*, vol. 38, part I, 423; Hazen, *Autobiography*, 258; Briant, *History of the Sixth*, 320; Johnston, *Four Months in Libby*, 164–65.

190. *Official Records*, vol. 38, part I, 435, 442.

CHAPTER 12

191. Cope, *The Fifteenth Ohio Volunteers*, 451.

192. Crowell, "The General Wept."

193. *Official Records*, vol. 38, part I, 378; Howard. *Autobiography*, 552–53; Wood, "Pickett's Mill."

194. *Official Records*, vol. 38, part I, 392, 413, 424; Franklin, "The Pickett's Mill Affair"; McMahon, "Pickett's Mills."

195. *Official Records*, vol. 38, part I, 442; Oliphant, *Only a Private*, 65; Young, "Letter."

196. *Official Records*, vol. 38, part I, 402, 418.

197. Young, "Letter"; Franklin, The Pickett's Mill Affair."

198. Cope, *The Fifteenth Ohio Volunteers*, 451, 454.

199. Young, "Letter"; Cope, *The Fifteenth Ohio Volunteers*, 451.

200. Cope, *The Fifteenth Ohio Volunteers*, 451; *Official Records*, vol. 38, part I, 413; Franklin, "The Pickett's Mill Affair"; Kiene, *Diary*, 229. Kiene describes the line of men in front of the 49th Ohio as "three regiments deep." That would certainly appear to be more than just remnants of Hazen's men maintaining the line. Of course, Kiene could have been mistaken in the confusion of battle, but I decided to take his word.

201. *Official Records*, vol. 38, part I, 406–07; Cope, *The Fifteenth Ohio Volunteers*, 451–52.

202. *Official Records*, vol. 38, part I, 407, Cope, *The Fifteenth Ohio Volunteers*, 452–54.

203. Cope, *The Fifteenth Ohio Volunteers*, 455.

204. Ibid., 452.

205. Cope, *The Fifteenth Ohio Volunteers*, 452–53; Howard, *Autobiography*, 555. In Howard's account of his wounding, he states that while he was walking, a fragment ricocheted off the ground before penetrating the bottom of his boot while his foot was in the up-step.

206. Kiene, *Diary*, 229.

207. Oliphant, *Only a Private*, 65.

208. *Official Records*, vol. 38, part I, 392, 402, 407; Cope, *The Fifteenth Ohio Volunteers*, 454–55.

CHAPTER 13

209. *History of the Seventy-Ninth*, 141; According to the United States Naval Observatory (USNO), sunset on May 27, 1864, occurred at 7:42 p.m., while full darkness fell at approximately 8:11 p.m.

210. *Official Records*, vol. 38, part I, 865–66; Howard, *Autobiography*, 555–56.

211. *Official Records*, vol. 38, part I, 379.

212. *Official Records*, vol. 38, part I, 447; Noe, *A Southern Boy in Blue*, 291; Barnes, *The Eighty-Sixth Regiment*, 364.

213. *Official Records*, vol. 38, part I, 472.

214. Kiene, *Diary*, 229.

215. *Official Records*, vol. 38, part I, 467, 472.

216. *Official Records*, vol. 38, part III, 725; Richey, *Tirailleurs*, 141–42.

217. *Official Records*, vol. 38, part I, 467; Noe, *A Southern Boy in Blue*, 292. It's entirely possible that the 79th Indiana and 19th Ohio arrived at the same time as the 9th Kentucky and helped repulse the 4th Louisiana, but only Woodcock in his memoirs mentions arriving and pushing back Confederate troops already in the cornfield. This provides some evidence to substantiate the arrival of the 9th Kentucky ahead of the other two.

218. *Official Records*, vol. 38, part I, 467, 475; *History of the Seventy-Ninth*, 141. It's possible that some or all of the 9th also advanced to the edge of the "shelf" in the cornfield, but neither Woodcock nor the 9th's report

mentions it. The 9th was definitely intermingled with the 17th, the left of which was in the ravine to the left, so absent any other evidence, they probably did not. Both the 79th and 19th Ohio mention taking rails from a fence, entering a field and making a barricade. We must assume this to be the cornfield. If they were in the large wheat field in front of Govan, they would have been subject to direct fire from the guns in Hotchkiss's Battalion, and neither of them mentioned being the target of such. In addition, the 86th Indiana, which was stationed at the far end of the large wheat field and was indeed the target of Hotchkiss's guns, does not mention any friendly forces in the field ahead of them.

219. Barnes, *The Eighty-Sixth Regiment*, 865.

220. *History of the Seventy-Ninth*, 141; Noe, *A Southern Boy in Blue*, 292–93, 330.

221. Lewis, *Campaigns of the 124th*, 151; Foster, *One of Cleburne's Command*, 85.

CHAPTER 14

222. *Official Records*, vol. 38, part I, 407; Cope, *The Fifteenth Ohio Volunteers*, 453–56. The 15th probably rallied at the Leverette house.

223. *Official Records*, vol. 38, part I, 414; Kiene, *Diary*, 229–30.

224. *Official Records*, vol. 38, part I, 402.

225. Oliphant, *Only a Private*, 65. While not mentioned explicitly, the colonel of the 32nd was Colonel Frank Erdelmeyer.

226. Collins, *Unwritten History*, 213; Lewis, *Campaigns of the 124th*, 151.

227. *Official Records*, vol. 38, part I, 460, 467–68; Noe, *A Southern Boy in Blue*, 293.

228. *Official Records*, vol. 38, part III, 725; Collins, *Unwritten History*, 213–14; Joslyn, *Meteor Shining Brightly*, 227. One soldier in Granbury's Brigade, Sergeant Asa G. Anderson of the 7th Texas, reported in a postwar reminiscence that General Granbury was wounded about 6:00 p.m., at which point Colonel Roger Q. Mills of the 10th Texas took over command. This is certainly possible, but Granbury must have recovered quickly and resumed command before sending Captain English to Cleburne asking for permission to attack. Cleburne's report makes no mention of his wounding—neither do any of the contemporary letters written during the war nor any of the personal biographies such as those of Collins and Foster. I chose to leave it out of the narrative due to this lack of corroborating evidence. Yearly, *Reminiscences of the Boys in Gray*, 18.

229. Jarman, "History of Company K," 2; *Official Records*, vol. 38, part III, 725.

230. Foster, *One of Cleburne's Command*, 85

231. Brandley, "Lively Times for Co. C."

232. Lewis, *Campaigns of the 124th*, 151–52. It may seem odd that the quartet would essentially ignore the living wounded and concentrate on removing the body of a dead man. It illustrates that the soldiers we read about on paper are not perfect, ideal heroes; they are flesh-and-blood men with their own motivations, desires and faults. Also, we do not know the condition of the wounded men they left behind. Perhaps they were too far gone to help or in no condition to be moved. Lewis did, in fact, feel guilt over the decision but placed the blame on Howard for not moving forward a skirmish line to cover them while they removed the dead and wounded. The blame is obviously misplaced, as Knefler's brigade did just that. However, with the brigade split between the ravine and the cornfield, the position of the 124th was probably in the gap between the two.

233. *Official Records*, vol. 38, part III, 725.

234. Lewis, *Campaigns of the 124th*, 153.

235. Foster, *One of Cleburne's Command*, 85–86; *Official Records*, vol. 38, part I, 472.

236. Foster, *One of Cleburne's Command*, 86; Spurlin, *Diary of Charles A. Leuschner*, 35.

237. *Official Records*, vol. 38, part III, 725–26; *Official Records*, vol. 38, part I, 460, 468, 475; Noe, *A Southern Boy in Blue*, 293.

238. Richards, *Saint Helena Rifles*, 20.

239. *Official Records*, vol. 38, part I, 595; Scribner, *How Soldiers Were Made*, 242.

240. *Official Records*, vol. 38, part I, 595; Scribner, *How Soldiers Were Made*, 242–43. It is interesting to note that Scribner makes no mention of meeting with Stout and refusing to advance his skirmish line in order to link up with Stout at the cornfield and that Stout makes no mention of meeting with Scribner during his retreat.

241. *Official Records*, vol. 38, part I, 615; Scribner, *How Soldiers Were Made*, 243. In his autobiography, Scribner makes it sound as if he had Given [last name of the commander of the 74th Ohio regiment] deploy his entire regiment to the right, but his actual report (as well as Given's) makes it clear that only Company A extended the line past the right of the 78th Pennsylvania. The remainder of the 74th probably moved behind the 78th in support, if it was not already there.

CHAPTER 15

242. *Official Records*, vol. 38, part I, 595; Scribner, *How Soldiers Were Made*, 243–44.

243. *Official Records*, vol. 38, part I, 595–96; Scribner, *How Soldiers Were Made*, 244–45.

244. Foster, *One of Cleburne's Command*, 86.

245. Lewis, *Campaigns of the 124th*, 154–55.

246. Howard, *Autobiography*, 555–56

247. Gay, *Life in Dixie*, 89–90.

248. Richards, *Saint Helena Rifles*, 24.

249. Smith, *Diary*, May 27, 1864.

250. Official Records, vol. 38, part I, 195, 392–93.

CHAPTER 16

251. Oliphant, *Only a Private*, 63; Bigbie, Letter to Wife.

252. Collins, *Unwritten History*, 215; Ridley, "Battle of New Hope Church," 460.

253. Oliphant, *Only a Private*, 63; Collins, *Unwritten History*, 215–16.

254. Richey, *Tirailleurs*, 143; Lundberg, *Granbury's Texas Brigade*, 155–56.

255. Sneed, Letter to Wife; Foster, *One of Cleburne's Command*, 88; Oliphant, *Only a Private*, 64.

256. Spurlin, *Diary of Charles A. Leuschner*, 35; Collins, *Unwritten History*, 215.

257. Lewis, *Campaigns of the 124th*, 155; Cope, *The Fifteenth Ohio Volunteers*, 453, 475; Johnson, *A Soldier's Reminiscence*, 279.

258. Noe, *A Southern Boy in Blue*, 294–95, 298.

259. *Official Records*, vol. 38, part I, 387; *Official Records*, vol. 38, part III, 726, 948–49. The eight casualties suffered by the artillery earlier in the day are not counted in the total for the battle.

260. *Official Records*, vol. 38, part I, 387, 413–14, 437; Franklin, "The Pickett's Mill Affair"; Walker, "Letter."

261. *Official Records*, vol. 38, part I, 596.

262. *Official Records*, vol. 38, part III, 726, 949; Richey, *Tirailleurs*, 143.

263. Cooper, *William Babcock Hazen*, 270–76; Briant, *History of the Sixth*, 317.

264. Official Records, vol. 38, part I, 113. The order relieving and transferring McLean is not included in the *Official Records*, so there is no way of knowing

exactly why Sherman transferred McLean. Howard and Sherman were on good terms, and Howard undoubtedly voiced his displeasure with McLean. McLean was the senior brigade commander in the Twenty-Third Corps at the time, and a promotion to command a division in a backwater command is a classic example of being "kicked upstairs."

CHAPTER 17

265. Secrist, *Sherman's 1864 Trail*, 83–87.
266. Dickens Jr. and Worthy. *Archaeological Investigations*, 8–13; *Official Records*, vol. 38, part I, 387.

APPENDIX

267. *Official Records*, vol. 38, part VI, 601–02.
268. Newton, *Lost for the Cause*, 21–23.
269. *Official Records*, vol. 38, part VI, 361. The figure is a best guess derived by taking the strength reported on May 30 and adding back in casualties where reported. It is not 100 percent accurate, but it's closer than using the May 2 returns, which are the only previous returns available for the division.
270. *Official Records*, vol. 38, part I, 402.
271. Ibid., 407
272. *Official Records*, vol. 38, part I, 413–14; Franklin, "The Pickett's Mill Affair." The official report lists "400 effective men." Franklin states that there were 414 men, which probably includes the 400 enlisted men and 14 officers.
273. Briant, *History of the Sixth*, 311, 320–21. Since this was derived from the muster rolls, it undoubtedly includes everyone present, or "Present for Duty."
274. Official Records, vol. 38, part I, 437.
275. Ibid., 439.
276. Ibid., 442.
277. Ibid., 454.
278. Ibid., 460.
279. Ibid., 468.
280. Ibid., 472.

281. Ibid., 475.

282. Ibid., 479.

283. Barnes, *The Eighty-Sixth Regiment*, 369.

284. *Official Records*, vol. 38, part I, 596.

285. Ibid., 608.

286. Ibid., 612–13. Number is derived from adding casualties back from report of July 9. Not accurate, but close.

287. Ibid., 596

288. A best guess.

289. Official Records, vol. 38, part II, 593. Strength from Resaca minus casualties.

290. Ibid., 599. Strength from Resaca minus casualties.

291. *Official Records*, vol. 38, part III, 726, 676. Cleburne reported "4,683 muskets," which would exclude officers and, possibly, NCO file closers. The division began the campaign with 540 officers. Officer casualties since the beginning of the campaign are not reported, so I added 530 to Cleburne's number.

292. Ibid., 731. Figure is from April 1, 1864, and is listed as "Present and Absent" but is probably closer to "Present for Duty."

293. *Official Records*, vol. 38, part III, 794–99. Strength from Resaca minus casualties.

294. Ibid.

295. Ibid.

296. Ibid.

297. Official Records, vol. 38, part III, 860. Figure for 30th Louisiana added to total as it was reported in another brigade at the time.

298. Kendall, "Fourth Louisiana Volunteers," 212.

299. Ibid.

300. *Official Records*, vol. 38, part III, 948. Figure in parentheses is the sum of the Present for Duty numbers reported for each brigade at the beginning of the campaign.

301. Kelly's Division also included the brigade commanded by Colonel George G. Dibrell. However, unlike Allen and Hannon, there are no primary sources that definitively place the brigade along the ridge at Pickett's Mill. Therefore, I have left the brigade off the order of battle and out of the narrative, as I cannot prove it was present at the battle.

302. *Official Records*, vol. 38, part III, 866.

303. Newton, *Lost for the Cause*, 265–66, 275.

Bibliography

Barnes, James A., James R. Carnahan, and Thomas H.B. McCain. *The Eighty-Sixth Regiment, Indiana Volunteer Infantry: A Narrative of its Services in the Civil War of 1861–1865*. Crawfordville, IN: The Journal Company Printers, 1895.

Beatty, John. *The Citizen-Soldier; or, Memoirs of a Volunteer*. Cincinnati, OH: Wilstach, Baldwin & Company, 1879.

Beszedits, Stephen. "Frederick Knefler: Hungarian Patriot and American General." *Jewish-American History Documentation Foundation*. http://www.jewish-history.com/civilwar/knefler.html.

Bierce, Ambrose. *The Collected Works of Ambrose Bierce*. Vol. 1. New York: The Neale Publishing Company, 1909.

Bigbie, Thomas T. Letter to Wife. May 29, 1864. Pickett's Mill Battlefield Historic Site Library, Folder 15. Dallas, GA.

Bigger, David Dwight. *Ohio's Silver-Tongued Orator: Life and Speeches of General William H. Gibson*. Dayton, OH: United Brethren Publishing house, 1901.

Bourne, Edward. "Govan's Brigade at New Hope Church." *Confederate Veteran* 31, no. 3 (March 1923): 89–90.

Brandley, Arnold. "Lively Times for Co. C, 23d Ky., at New Hope Church." *National Tribune*, December 17, 1896.

Briant, C.C. *History of the Sixth Regiment Indiana Volunteer Infantry*. Indianapolis, IN: Wm B. Buford, Printer and Binders, 1891.

Brock, R.A., ed. *Southern Historical Society Papers* 16. Richmond, VA: William Ellis Jones, 1888.

Calkins, William Wirt. *The History of the One Hundred and Fourth Regiment of Illinois Volunteer Infantry. War of the Great Rebellion 1862–1865*. Chicago: Donohue & Henneberry, 1895.

Castel, Albert. *Decision in the West: The Atlanta Campaign of 1864*. Lawrence: University Press of Kansas, 1992.

Collins, R.M. *Chapters from the Unwritten History of the War Between the States; or, The Incidents in the Life of a Confederate Soldier in Camp, on the March, in the Great Battles, and in Prison*. Dayton, OH: Morningside house, Inc., 1988.

Cooper, Edward S. *William Babcock Hazen: The Best Hated Man*. Cranbury, NJ: Associated University Press, 2005.

Cope, Alexis. *The Fifteenth Ohio Volunteers and Its Campaigns, War of 1861–65*. Columbus, OH: The Blade Printing Co., 1901.

Cox, Jacob Dolson. *Military Reminiscences of the Civil War*. Vol. 1 New York: Charles Scribner's Sons, 1900.

Cozzens, Peter. *This Terrible Sound: The Battle of Chickamauga*. Chicago: University of Illinois Press, 1992.

Crowell, Silas. "The General Wept." *National Tribune*, December 31, 1896.

Dickens, Roy S., Jr., and Linda H. Worthy. *Archaeological Investigations at Pickett's Mill Historic Site: Paulding County Georgia*. 2nd ed. Edited by John R. Morgan. Atlanta: State of Georgia Department of Natural Resources, 1984.

Duff, A.J. Letter to his Aunt Teresa. May 29, 1864. Pickett's Mill Battlefield Historic Site Library, Folder 15. Dallas, GA.

Dyer, Frederick H. *A Compendium of the War of the Rebellion*. Des Moines: The Dyer Publishing Company, 1908.

Foster, Samuel T. *One of Cleburne's Command: The Civil War Reminiscences and Diary of Capt. Samuel T. Foster, Granbury's Texas Brigade, CSA*. Edited by Norman D. Brown. Austin: University of Texas Press, 1980.

Fowler, Jeff. *Jeff Fowler's Civil War Diary*. Pickett's Mill Battlefield Historic Site Library, Folder 15. Dallas, GA.

Fox, William F. *Regimental Losses in the American Civil War 1861–1865*. Albany, New York: Albany Publishing Company, 1889.

Franklin, W.S. "The Pickett's Mill Affair." *National Tribune*, February 17, 1898.

———. "Under a Terrible Fire." *National Tribune*, January 27, 1898.

Gay, Mary A.H. *Life in Dixie During the War: 1861–1862–1863–1864–1865*. Atlanta: Charles P. Byrd, 1897.

Gibson, J.T., ed. *History of the Seventy-Eighth Pennsylvania Volunteer Infantry*. Pittsburgh: Pittsburgh Printing Company, 1905.

Hamilton, Posey. "Battle of New Hope Church, Ga." *Confederate Veteran* 30, no. 9 (September 1922): 338–39.

Hay, Thomas R., ed. *Cleburne and His Command by Capt. Irving A. Buck, C.S.A.* Wilmington, NC: Broadfoot Publishing Company, 1987.

Hazen, William B. *A Narrative of Military Service*. Boston: Ticknor and Company, 1885.

Hennessy, John J. *Return to Bull Run: The Campaign and Battle of Second Manassas*. New York: Simon & Schuster, 1993.

History of the Seventy-Ninth Regiment Indiana Volunteer Infantry. Indianapolis, IN: The Hollenbeck Press, 1891.

Hoskins, I.W. "Scribner's Brigade" *National Tribune*, July 28, 1887.

Howard, Oliver Otis. *Autobiography of Oliver Otis Howard: Major General United States Army*. Vol. 1. New York: The Baker & Taylor Company, 1907.

Howe, M.A. DeWolfe. *Home Letters of General Sherman*. New York: Charles Scribner's Sons, 1909.

Hurley, Stan C. "Govan's Brigade at Pickett's Mill." *Confederate Veteran* 12, no. 2 (February 1904): 74–76.

Jarman, R.A. "The History of Company K, 27th Mississippi Infantry, Continued." *The Aberdeen Examiner* 21 March 1890): 2.

Johnson, Mark W. *That Body of Brave Men: The U.S. Regular Infantry in the Civil War in the West*. Cambridge, MA: Da Capo Press, 2003.

Johnson, Richard W. *A Soldier's Reminiscences in Peace and War*. Philadelphia: J.B. Lippincott Company, 1886.

Johnston, Isaac N. *Four Months in Libby, and the Campaign Against Atlanta*. Cincinnati: R.P. Thompson, 1864.

Johnston, Joseph E. *Narrative of Military Operations, Directed, During the Late War Between the States*. New York: D. Appleton and Company, 1874.

Joslyn, Mauriel Phillips, ed. *A Meteor Shining Brightly*. Milledgeville, GA: Terrell house, 1998.

Kendall, John S. "Fourth Louisiana Volunteers." *Confederate Veteran* 9, no. 5 (May 1901): 210–12. Kerksis, Sydney C. *The Atlanta Papers*. Dayton, OH: Morningside house, Inc., 1980.

Kiene, Ralph E., Jr. *A Civil War Diary: The Journal of Francis A. Kiene*. Privately published, 1974.

Kimberly, Robert L., and Ephraim S. Holloway. *The Forty-First Ohio Veteran Volunteer Infantry in the War of the Rebellion, 1861–1865.* Cleveland: W.R. Smellie, Printer and Publisher, 1897.

Lewis, G.W. *The Campaigns of the 124th Regiment Ohio Volunteer Infantry, With Roster and Honor Roll.* Akron, OH: The Werner Company, 1894.

Lundberg, John R. *Granbury's Texas Brigade: Diehard Western Confederates.* Baton Rouge: Louisiana State University Press, 2012.

McDermott, Gregory C. "A Fierce Hour at New Hope." *National Tribune,* October 28, 1897.

McMahon, James. "Pickett's Mills" *National Tribune,* November 25, 1886.

Members of the Battery. *History of the Organization, Marches, Campings, General Services and Final Muster Out of Battery M, First Regiment Illinois Light Artillery.* Princeton, IL: Mercer & Dean, 1892.

Newton, Steven H. *Lost for the Cause: The Confederate Army in 1864.* Mason City, IA: Savas Publishing Company, 2000.

Noe, Kenneth W. *A Southern Boy in Blue: The Memoir of Marcus Woodcock 9th Kentucky Infantry (U.S A.).* Knoxville: The University of Tennessee Press, 1996.

Oliphant, William J. *Only a Private: A Texan Remembers the Civil War: The Memoirs of William J. Oliphant.* Edited by James M. McCaffrey. Houston: Halycon Press, Ltd., 2004.

Otto, John Henry. *Capt. John Henry Ottos' Diary: 21st Wisconsin Infantry Regiment.* Pickett's Mill Battlefield Historic Site Library, Folder 10. Dallas, GA.

Owens, Ira S. *Green County Soldiers in the Late War: Being a History of the Seventy-Fourth O.V.I.* Dayton, OH: Christian Publishing house Print, 1884.

Perry, Henry Fales. *History of the Thirty-Eighth Regiment Indiana Volunteer Infantry.* Palo Alto, CA: F.A. Stuart, 1906.

Price, William N. *One Year in the Civil War: A Diary of the Events from April 1st, 1864, to April 1st, 1865.* Privately published, n.d.

Puntenney, George H. *History of the Thirty-Seventh Regiment Of Indiana Infantry Volunteers.* Rushville, IN: Jacksonian Book and Job Department, 1896.

Purdue, Howell, and Elizabeth Howell. *Pat Cleburne: Confederate General.* Hillsboro, TX: Hill Jr. College Press, 1973.

Reid, Whitelaw. *Ohio in the War: Her Statesmen, Her Generals, and Soldiers.* Cincinnati: Moore, Wilstach & Baldwin, 1868.

Richards, A.P. *The Saint Helena Rifles.* Edited by Randall Shoemaker. Houston: Privately published, 1968.

Richey, Thomas H. *Tirailleurs: A History of the 4th Louisiana and the Acadians of Company H.* Lincoln, NE: iUniverse, Inc., 2003.

Ridley, B.L. "The Battle of New Hope Church." *Confederate Veteran* 5, no. 9 (September 1897): 459–60.

Scribner, B.F. *How Soldiers Were Made; or, The War as I Saw It Under Buell, Rosecrans, Thomas, Grant, and Sherman.* New Albany, IN: Donohue & Henneberry, Printers and Binders, 1887.

Secrist, Philip L. *Sherman's 1864 Trail of Battles to Atlanta.* Macon, GA: Mercer University Press, 2006.

Sherman, William T. *Memoirs of General William T. Sherman.* Vol. 2. New York: D. Appleton and Company, 1875.

Smith, William Austin. *Diary of William Austin Smith.* Pickett's Mill Battlefield Historic Site Library, Folder 15. Dallas, GA.

Sneed, Sebron. Letter to Wife. May 27, 1964. Pickett's Mill Battlefield Historic Site Library, Folder 15. Dallas, GA.

Spurlin, Charles D. *The Civil War Diary of Charles A. Leuschner.* Austin, TX: Eakin Press, 1992.

Stahl, William. *Diary of William Stahl*. Pickett's Mill Battlefield Historic Site Library, Folder 14. Dallas, GA.

Starkweather, John C. *Statement of Military Services of Brigadier General John C. Starkweather, of Wisconsin, Since the 4th of March 1861*. Milwaukee: Daily Sentinel Print, 1864.

Sutherland, Daniel E., ed. *Reminiscences of a Private: William E. Bevens of the First Arkansas Infantry, C.S.A*. Fayetteville: The University of Arkansas Press, 1992.

U.S. War Department. *The War of the Rebellion: A Compilation of the Official Records of the Union and Confederate Armies*. 128 vols. Washington, D.C.: Government Printing Office, 1880–1901.

Walker, E.P. "Letter." *National Tribune*, May 23, 1889.

Warner, Ezra J. *Generals in Blue: The Lives of the Union Commanders*. Baton Rouge: Louisiana State University Press, 1992.

Watkins, Sam R. *"Co. Aytch," Maury Grays, First Tennessee Regiment; or, A Side Show of the Big Show*. Chattanooga, TN: Times Printing Company, 1900.

Wheeler's Confederate Cavalry Association. *Campaigns of Wheeler and His Cavalry 1862-1865*. Edited by W.C. Dodson. Atlanta: Hudgins Publishing Company, 1899.

Willis, Riley. *Old Enough to Die*. Franklin, TN: Hillsboro Press, 1996.

Wood, Thomas J. "Pickett's Mill" *National Tribune*, December 22, 1897.

Yeary, Maime, ed. *Reminiscences of the Boys in Gray, 1861–1865*. Dallas, TX: Smith & Lamar Publishing house, 1912.

Young, Isaac K. "Letter." *Aurora Beacon*, June 16, 1864.

Index

Y

About the Author

Brad Butkovich has a BA in history from Georgia Southern University. Having spent more than a decade in the role-playing game publishing industry, he took time off to be a stay-at-home parent and is now an account executive at American 3B Scientific. A member of the Northeast Georgia Civil War Round Table and the Civil War Trust, he has published several books on American Civil War miniature gaming and enjoys painting historic miniatures and plastic models. His keen interest in Civil War history, photography and cartography recently came together in the launching of the Civil War Virtual Tours website, which provides detailed views of several battles and engagements.